CHANCE ENCOUNTERS

Life Lessons We Learn From People We Don't Even Know

Dr. Michael B. Brown

To all the friends whose names I never knew, but whose momentary interactions with me changed the way I see the world ... Thank You!

And with gratitude to my wife, Page, who knows me as I am and loves me anyway.

Contents

CHANCE ENCOUNTERS

*Life Lessons We Learn From People We
Don't Even Know*

Preface

Part of the vernacular of society is the term "angels unaware" (a biblical phrase originally appearing in Hebrews 13:2). In most religious thought, including but not limited to Judaism and Christianity, angels are simply "God's messengers" (bearers of divine Truth), and messengers can take many forms. I can sense Truth in new or refreshed ways from poets and prophets, theology and theater, mystics and music, history and humor, philosophy and philanthropy, artists and activists, coaches and cooks, and the list goes on. From men and women, from the very young or the very old, from liberals or conservatives, from those like myself or often from those who are very different, and from persons of all philosophical systems or political persuasions, I gain insights into things of genuine significance.

Frequently, I find that some bit of understanding penetrates when I least expect it. Usually, the reason I don't expect it on those particular occasions is because the insight is the result of a momentary chance encounter with someone I do not know. Our worlds connect briefly, in all likelihood never to connect again, but something happens that changes me. An epiphany occurs. There is a takeaway that causes me to see new Truth or to remember old Truth too long forgotten. Those strangers become mystic messengers to me, angels both unexpected and unaware.

This book is a personal collection of such brief encounters. It is my habit to record things that get my attention. I bump into someone. Something occurs as a result of it, something that is out of the ordinary, beyond the norm. Not much time will elapse before I write down the nature of the encounter and the emotion(s) I felt when it happened. Then, from time to time, I read and re-read that record of encounters and remember the Truth(s) that resulted from them. In this book, I simply share some of those moments with you. Perhaps they will reveal the same Truths to you that I perceived. Perhaps they will reveal insights I never recognized at all. In any event, may these stories and my reflections upon them provide you with whatever muses you may need at this point in your journey. Read happily, and be open to the magnificent mystery of chance encounters.

The Man on the Landing

"Out of the depths I cry to you, Lord ... hear my voice.

Let your ears be attentive to my cry for mercy."

(Psalm 130:1-2,

New International Version)

A person can see almost every slice of the demographic pie on subway landings in New York City. I spent a lot of time and did a lot of people-watching on those landings during my ten years as a resident of the city. At any given moment, you would see a hurried mother taking her child to a pediatrician's office, an elderly couple going to a different office nearby, afraid of the diagnosis one of them might receive, a well-dressed businesswoman on her way to the Financial District, a street-dweller who often sleeps in unseen subway caverns, students headed off to NYU or Hunter College, tourists with maps directing them to Time Square or the site of the Twin Towers, and all manners of others who live in the city and use those rails to get from here to there. We observe our daily ritual of gathering in shoulder-to-shoulder silence, waiting for the trains. We are a microcosm of all humanity on those landings, rich and poor, with every hue and color, every philosophy and religion, every dream and disappointment, all waiting to be taken to one place or away from another. Usually, what we have in common is our sense of isolation, a community of strangers touching shoulders but avoiding eye contact.

When, however, we dare to look or listen while on those landings or in those trains, we see more than diversity. We see human reality, sometimes even raw emotion, that for a brief moment drops its disguises.

At the end of a long, hot summer's day, I walked down the steps to wait for the Six Train. Though the trains are air-conditioned, the landings are not. When the wait is long, it can be like standing in a sauna. That day, the wait was just long enough to make most of us feel even more uncomfortable and weary than we already felt.

Leaning against a pillar was a man who looked like my concept of Willy Loman (the key

character in Arthur Miller's *Death of a Salesman*).
He was dressed in a seersucker suit that was
wrinkled from a long day's wear, perhaps from
many days' wear between trips to the dry
cleaner's. His thinning hair was disheveled. His
tie had been loosened. You could see the
dampness of the August heat sweating its way
through his aging white shirt. His worn and
weathered briefcase, which appeared to have
suffered through many years of similar
journeys with him, sat at his feet on the landing.

Our eyes met for just a moment. Usually, we
subway riders try to avoid allowing that to
happen, much the same as people do on
elevators. Just look at the numbers as the floors
change. Pretend no one else is riding up or
down with you. And soon, if you're lucky, the
door will open and you can exit without having
to endure human contact at all. Elevators and
subway landings have that in common. But, his
eyes met mine. And when they did, he spoke. It
was just a single sentence. A total stranger
looked me in the eye and said, "I am so tired."
With that, the train arrived, the doors opened,
and both of us entered. I stood at one end of the
car. He found a seat at the other. We exchanged
no further words or glances. Three stops later, I
exited the train and walked home.

"I am so tired." Was it a commentary on his day or on his life? Had he just received the bad news of being downsized? Perhaps he had worked for the same firm for thirty years. But now, with children still in college, a mortgage not yet paid, and retirement looming on the not-too-distant but not-yet-fully-funded horizon, the end of the day had unexpectedly included the end of his employment. Where do you go at fifty-five or sixty? How do you compete with the young grads fresh out of Stanford, Duke, or Yale? How do you find the energy to market yourself or, if fortunate enough to be hired, to start over? And, how about those at home who are waiting for you to arrive in time for dinner? "Hello, sweetheart," she says with a smile. "Tell me about your day." How do you answer this aging lover who depends on you, who has trusted you to provide for the family? How do you confess that after all these years and all this work, you have no idea where the next paycheck is coming from? Down deep, whatever your pedigree or track record, at that moment, you feel like a failure. "I am so tired."

Or was it physical fatigue he expressed, the worn-out-down-to-the-soul feeling of working long hours and seeing little results? Had he pounded Manhattan's pavements all day, knocking on doors but rarely getting to see the persons who could award the contracts or buy the products? Was there a quota that had to be met, and now two-thirds of the month was gone and he still had not made his first sale? When we try and try and keep on trying but come up empty, at some point we feel tired. "Worn-out-down-to-the-soul." We have hit a wall. There's nothing left. We don't believe we can make it over the next hill and the one after that, but we have no option but to try. Willy Loman has to return to the subways and sidewalks and waiting rooms again the next day, knowing before he does what the ultimate outcome is likely to be. How do you keep your chin up living a life like that? How do you maintain enough confidence to achieve even minor successes? Where our emotions go, our bodies follow. Totally exhausted, he stands on a subway landing and says to a stranger, "I am so tired." He's being honest. His body reminds him what his soul is feeling.

Perhaps, though, he was not so much "tired" as "tired of." Tired of the rat race. Tired of the routine. Tired of stretching the truth to make a sale. Tired of having to live according to the ethics of a supervisor who, he feels, is profoundly unethical. Tired of being chastised for not doing enough, not being enough. Tired of the noises on the streets—the sirens, the vulgar voices yelling their anger into cell phones, the blaring horns of taxis passing by. Maybe not that long ago, he and his family spent a week in a rented cottage on the coast of Long Island, Maryland, or the Outer Banks. But now he knew that ten more months would pass before he could go barefoot again, before he could sleep late on Tuesday mornings or have a margarita before bed. Day by day, he would be up at 6:30, out the door by 7:30, walking the pavement, riding the subways, and finally home by 8:00 pm, only to do it again the day after that. Was he eight weeks out from his last vacation and already fatigued, with over forty weeks remaining before his next one?

Or, was he tired of someone? Had the magic gone from a relationship that refused to go? Perhaps there was not someone waiting over dinner, gently saying, "Tell me about your day." Perhaps, instead, someone he no longer knew was living under the same roof, someone as tired of him as he was of her, someone whose eyes and arms were closed and cold. There was no passion except the passion of anger. There was little conversation except the conversation of mundane matters that served no purpose except to soften the oppressive silence. Even that often resulted in critique or argument. He remembered being young and impulsive, given to romance and longings, but those were distant memories for him and, also, for her. Perhaps too many years with too much stress and too little time and effort set aside to nurture love had left them both "tired of" being together but unsure how to fix it and too weary to walk away. "I am so tired."

"I am so tired." I have no idea what he meant, but I am aware that the statement can mean myriad things. It can refer to the body but also to the psyche. It can reflect where we are in life as opposed to where we had hoped to be. It can reflect where we fear we may wind up. I have no idea what was behind his words. But I believed him when the weary-looking man in the wrinkled suit said, "I am so tired."

Why did he share that word with someone he neither knew nor would ever encounter again? If you are worn out by something or with someone and need to plan a strategy to make things better, aren't you best advised to seek counsel? You go to a trusted friend, a life coach, a professional adviser, a clergyperson, or a therapist. You lay all the cards on the table. A trained listener helps you look at things from every angle. You weigh realities and assess alternatives. "Option A isn't working for me. Should I try Option B?" "But if you try Option B, have you thought about the consequences?

Maybe you should try Option C." And so it goes until your insights, alongside the other person's advice, jointly map a plan to move from fatigue to renewal. But Mr. Loman on the platform shared the weight that was bearing down on his soul with a stranger. He mentioned his pain to me and then turned and was absorbed into the mass of people on a train. He didn't even give me a chance to respond, nor would I have known exactly what to say if he had. Our worlds had never collided before and would not do so in the future. It was one brief, painful, poignant moment when a stranger said to another stranger, "I am so tired."

So, was Willy Loman illustrating the truth for me that there are times when simply naming the demon is enough? We do not necessarily want advice. We resist sermons. We deplore pontificating. We simply want to speak and be heard. Sometimes, that is sufficient in a given specific moment. We just need to name our pain and have someone acknowledge it. For in so doing, they acknowledge us. In that moment, he was more than a stick figure on a subway landing. Our eyes made contact. He spoke to me his own deep and disturbing truth about his own very personal journey. He revealed to me who he essentially was, at least in that place and moment in time. He said to another human being, "Look at me! Take me into account! Know me by my reality if not by my name. Hear my confession, and let that be enough. Then I can walk away knowing that for one minute during the day, it was all about me. I was no longer selling anything to anybody. I was no longer living up to unrealistic expectations. I was simply pulling back the curtains and asking someone to gaze upon the inner reality of my heart."

As I walked the rest of the way home that afternoon, reflecting on the man on the landing, *my takeaway had to do with the power of listening*. Perhaps even more, it had to do with the power of being heard, of being taken seriously. He apparently was not asking anyone to fix his life nor to advise him how that should be done. Had that been the case, he would have sought professional counsel. In a big, overwhelming city of eight million people where most of us were lost in the crowd much of the time, he simply wanted to be heard. "Look at me! Listen to me! Hear my pain, and in hearing, remind me that I am not invisible!"

It was not the first time I had learned that lesson, but it was a reminder of a lesson too easily forgotten. When my sons were very small, they would often sit with me on the sofa, one on either side. Each son had the same habit.

If the television were on, sometimes I would be more aware of it than of them. Looking back, I recognize the foolishness of that and too many other lost moments. But my sons were committed to taking whatever action was required to prevent moments from being lost. When either child tried to talk to daddy, and if daddy mumbled a response while fixated on the TV screen, the child doing the speaking would take my face in his hands and literally turn my gaze to him. It was a child's way of saying what the man on the subway landing said. "Look at me. Listen to me. Take me seriously. Remind me that I matter, that I am not invisible." While making the slow walk down 51st Street, I recalled those moments with fragile children longing to be taken into account. And I wondered if I had just encountered another such person in a wrinkled seersucker suit on the 28th Street landing. "I am so tired," he said to a stranger. Was that his way of taking someone's face into his hands and turning their gaze in his direction? Was it his plaintive cry to be noticed, to be heard, and thus to be reminded that he was not actually alone?

So many of us who spend our lives in helping professions are just codependent enough to misinterpret that word: "help." We feel we have helped another only by curing their ills. We have assisted only when we resolve their problems or repair their broken issues. But, not all problems can be that easily resolved. The greatest problem may, in fact, be the mere question of existence: "Does anyone notice that I'm here? Does anyone take me into account?" And that we can address simply through the discipline of hearing.

Hearing is, of course, more than simply listening. I can listen to a song without paying attention to its words. I can listen to a scream from a neighboring apartment without sufficient data to know if it is a cry of pain or a cry of joy. I can listen to passing cars without knowing where they are headed or why. I can listen to you without paying full attention, and your story will sound like little more than the unintelligible droning of Charlie Brown's school teacher in the *Peanuts* TV cartoons. To *hear* someone is to listen with the intent of understanding. It is empathy in action. It does not promise to fix or repair, but it does promise to acknowledge and take seriously.

There are small actions that let others know they are being heard. If eye contact is not at the head of the list, it is certainly close. Without speaking, our eyes communicate. They express sympathy or compassion, anger or surprise, kindness or intrigue. To look at someone is to affirm that they exist, that they are seen and even valued. Willy Loman and I made eye contact on the subway platform. And if nothing else occurred, at least for a brief moment, the man no longer felt invisible.

Certain phrases accomplish the same. He and I had no time for that. But had we been given a minute or two, I could have said, "What do you mean by that?" or "I'd like to hear more," or "I hear you saying that…" In those simple phrases, it is possible that he would have felt "heard." To be heard is to be acknowledged. It is to be considered. It is to be affirmed as having an opinion of interest. When one's idea is heard and acknowledged, the person feels valued as a human being. A friend who is a counselor told me once, "What my clients need to know most of all is simply that they matter." Short phrases sincerely spoken communicate that to another. "Tell me more" can be like a love whisper, reminding someone that they really do matter after all.

I often looked for him when I took the Six Train in the afternoons. Our paths, however, never crossed again. His life moved in its directions, and mine did the same. My genuine hope is that someone will have the extra moment that I did not have to truly hear him and, in so doing, to remind him that he does not make the journey alone. Perhaps someone will be able to surprise him with the good news that he matters. My fantasy is that I could someday have that opportunity, that one hot afternoon, he will be leaning once more against the pillar on the 28th Street landing, disheveled and alone, and our eyes will meet again. But this time, I will be the first one to speak. If so, I think I will simply say, "Tell me about it." And maybe he will. Or maybe it will be enough just to know that someone was interested.

This much I do know. That chance encounter was a reminder of Truth to me, the truth that, ultimately, people need to be seen and heard. At the end of the day, seeing and hearing may be all I can do for them. But, it may be enough.

Santa In Shorts And Sandals

"Blessed are the peacemakers, for they will be called children of God."

(Matthew 5:9,

New International Version)

The further south I travel in winter, the more okay I am with it from the standpoint of weather. During one particular mid-December I was feeling very much okay, seated at a sidewalk café on Ocean Drive in Miami, watching people swim in the warm waters of the Atlantic. I had just left a beautiful place which I loved dearly. But when I flew out of that beautiful place, the temperatures were in the low 20s and falling. South Miami in December was working out just fine for me.

Each day for a week, while my wife was attending a continuing education event, I enjoyed lunches at a series of cafés on that famous strip. The rich and famous play there at night. But during the daytime, we mere mortals set up shop. Amidst the boutiques, wine bars, and coffee shops are scores of lovely restaurants that offer enjoyable cuisine and a view of the ocean. So day by day, I sat there, reading the Miami Herald, slowly savoring omelets or Cuban sandwiches with an occasional slice of key lime pie, and people-watching. The latter (watching the locals and tourists experiencing life) may have been the tastiest treat of all because people are undeniably fascinating if we pay attention.

Admittedly, as with tasty food, people-watching has its share of both sweet and savory. Not every human story is a happy one. That doesn't mean it is disinteresting. It simply means that when we watch one another closely, we see smiles *and* tears, joys *and* sorrows, victories *and* challenges, plenty *and* want. Between Ocean Drive and the beach is Lummus Park, a beautiful public space that has served as the backdrop for countless beach movies. It has outdoor fitness areas and a long, white beach for volleyball, tossing Frisbees, and sunning. There is laughter there. The park is inhabited by families and students and lovers on their way to the beach, by police who are present to ensure everyone's safety, by children who play under the careful watch of grandma and grandpa, and by anyone who wants to step away from the race and rush of life to just stroll or saunter for a bit. It is also a spot where hungry people look through trash containers for portions of sandwiches or croissants that others have discarded. When it's warm and dry enough to do so, some who have no place to call home nap on the park's benches because it is visible and safe there. The poor are there, as they are everywhere. And, for those who have eyes to see, the poor are visible to individuals on the rich side of the street. In fact, it's impossible to look at the sea from the other side of Ocean Drive without seeing the people who exist between the boutiques and the blue-green waves.

Each day, as I sat at cafés or walked through the park, I spotted the same man. Apparently he had a lunchtime mission. We never met, but I saw him daily at lunch time. I watched as he walked along that street. And I watched others as they watched him. The man was short and round with a belly that I am certain "shook when he laughed like a bowl full of jelly." He had not-quite-shoulder-length white hair and a full but well-trimmed white beard. He wore shorts, a t-shirt, and sandals appropriate for the warm weather. Atop his head was a bright red

Santa's cap. Day by day, he walked down Ocean Drive, looking to both sides, waving at individuals of all ages, and saying: "Peace, my man!" "Peace, lovely lady!" "Peace!"

At a small café during one of my lunches, I sat at an outdoor table finishing a delicious sandwich and salad. There he came again as regular as clockwork, the Santa-in-shorts offering his gift to all. On that day, he looked right at me (or, at least, to me it seemed that he did) and said with his broad smile, "Peace, my man!" It happened that a table server was present at that moment, refilling my glass of tea. So I asked, "Who is that unusual fellow?" The young man answered, "He's Santa." I chuckled and then continued, "Yeah, I know who he looks like. But, do you know who he actually is and why he does this every day?" The table server looked back at me without a trace of a smile and answered, "I told you. I think he's Santa. He shows up for everybody on this street. He smiles and waves at the rich and famous *and* at the poor and forgotten. He sees people on both sides of the street and treats them the same. It's like he gets it. He recognizes that however different people may appear, we all have similar needs and wounds and fears and loneliness. So, he offers all of us the gift of peace. Peace. If that's not Santa, who is?" With that, he smiled, turned, and made his way to the next table.

As I sat with my tea and my thoughts, watching Santa-in-shorts continue his one-man parade down the street offering his gift to strangers, two takeaways came to mind.

[1] Maybe one of our primary purposes in life is to bring joy.

It was undeniably obvious the bearded man in the red cap was doing that for the hungry searching through trash containers in Lummus Park. For a moment, when he called out his good wishes, they would pause their searches, look in his direction, wave and smile. In all likelihood, most of them had little to smile about. They were poor. Perhaps they had no place to sleep. They carried with them a litany of losses most of us could neither guess nor imagine, losses of homes, families, careers, health, self-esteem, hope. But for one brief moment all that was interrupted by joy. Santa's smile and intentional notice of them temporarily paused their pain. Maybe it took them back to other days as children, or with children of their own, other Christmas seasons when they had something to smile about. He did not magically erase the circumstances that had led them to where they were, nor did he change the world in which they found themselves rummaging through cans for half-eaten sandwiches others had thrown away. But for one brief instance, he restored their smiles. The gift of joy, even if momentary, at some deep level sets hope into motion. If I can find joy, however briefly, then I know that there is more joy to be found. And whenever one good person makes that happen, then I know there are other good people who can and will do the same.

There is all sorts of poverty. Who knows what litanies of pain or loss the more privileged people at the café tables carried in their hearts that day? No doubt many labored with physical pain, or guilt, or an awareness of living less-than-authentic lives, or broken relationships with children or spouses, or the creeping realization that they were having trouble discovering happiness no matter how many material possessions they accumulated, or worries about aging, or a kind of sadness that whispers of a lack of meaning in one's life. Maybe for some, their bank accounts were healthy, but their souls felt empty. But suddenly, a round, smiling, bearded man in sandals, shorts, and a Santa's cap looked them in the eye, saw something in them that they assumed no one could ever see, and made them smile again. Just for a moment, they actually smiled again. It is not unreasonable to think that the source of their smiles was exactly the same as was the case for their brothers and sisters on the other side of the street: memories of Christmases when they were children or had young children of their own and life had meaning and joy. Santa did not restore those times. But he did remind them of those times, and in so doing at least hinted to them that meaning and joy could still be found.

It could be that one of our primary purposes is to do what South Beach's Santa did—to bring moments of joy to people, moments when— through a word, a deed, or a gesture—we give them a reason to smile again. We can't change anyone's life, not essentially. But we can strengthen or encourage it. We can help others tap into the repressed or forgotten senses of hope that, if reawakened, can help people move from merely existing to actually living. And the good news is that when we sow seeds of joy in others, we reap that same harvest for ourselves. Happiness is the one thing we find only by giving it away. I would like to think that someone at a café table that day was inspired to do something for a person on the other side of the street and, in so doing, found a reason to smile that was more than momentary.

[2] Maybe one of our primary purposes in life is to offer peace.

In a world like ours, peacemakers really are blessed folks.

(Matthew 5:9)

In recorded human history, there have only been thirty years when some group was not waging war against some other group. As I write this chapter, there are over one hundred wars or armed conflicts being fought globally (Source: Geneva Academy). Most are waged as the result of a lust for land, oil, money, power, or all of the above. Many have religious or philosophical motives publicly attached, but the real motive is usually power and greed. The end result, of course, is that innocent people suffer and die.

Peace in too many places too much of the time is a foreign concept. In too many homes, too much of the time, peace is also difficult (and sometimes feels impossible) to find. And, in too many offices. In too many neighborhoods. Too many legislative assemblies. Too many political campaigns where self-serving candidates turned former friends, neighbors, and family members into enemies. In too many communities of faith. And, on too many campuses. In human relationships, when "I" takes precedence over "we," or "my" over "our," where cliques or exclusivity exist, where unkind words are frequently spoken or loving ones are consistently left unspoken, where insensitivity or competitiveness are given free reign, where bias or prejudice are allowed to take up residence, there is no peace. People suffer and die emotionally in ways not as visible as through bullets and bombs. But they still suffer and die on the inside.

In too many human hearts too much of the time, there is no peace. There may be respite, oases, brief moments when a bit of self-doubt is lifted, but those are exceptions rather than ongoing rules. Countless people live their lives in a slow burn of anxiety, fearing that they are somehow simply "not enough."

To a great extent, inner peace begins the moment you choose not to allow another person or event to control your emotions. In a PBS special I did entitled *5 Steps to a Loving and Purposeful Life* (PBS Television, 2020), my fifth and concluding point was: "Your Choices

Determine Your Outcome." In a somewhat prescriptive fashion, I articulated specific decisions anyone can make daily to improve the quality (and enhance the joy) of his or her personal life. My intent was simply to give people a helpful outline, more-or-less a starter kit, for designing a more meaningful life than they had thus far discovered. I did not anticipate the responses I received in reference to that particular one of the *5 Steps*. I heard from numerous people who said that designing their own future was practically a new concept to them. They wrote of how they had sought to live up to everyone's expectations but their own, how they had chased the dreams of others who had imposed those dreams upon them, how they had felt successful only when behaving well enough per someone else's standards to receive a figurative pat on the head. They wrote of how they had bought into the myth that peace results from earning more, receiving more, acquiring more. They wrote of being on treadmills they had not created and having no idea how to get off and fashion their own paths to a fulfilling life. All those stories reminded me of the truth about finding inner peace, and how (to quote the late Wayne Dyar) it frequently results from learning to "pull your own strings."

In a world where multitudes of people who surround us live lives of quiet desperation, it may well be that one of our primary purposes is to become conduits of peace as was that Santa on Ocean Drive. That can be accomplished in myriad ways: through what we advocate for, by what we work for on local levels, by how we carry ourselves in settings where we come shoulder-to-shoulder and soul-to-soul with others, by how we choose to encourage people to be themselves rather than impose upon them what we think those selves should look like, by how we offer that same grace to our own selves when we finally decide (in Joseph Campbell's words) to "follow our bliss" rather than to bow to someone else's expectations, and by how we choose to reinterpret what "success" means (finally realizing that it is ultimately not about what we have but rather about what we experience and what we give away).

"Peace, my man!" "Peace, lovely lady!" "Peace!" One of the beauties of that Santa is that he forced people on both sides of the street to see one another as they watched him—and to possibly set aside fear or prejudice and discover the sense of human oneness that makes us all family. Maybe the haves on the boutique side of the street, while seeing the have-nots so near and so real, found enough Christmas spirit to make a decision to do something for those who were having trouble doing it for themselves. And maybe those in need would, in time at least, begin to trust again that there are kind people in the world, potential friends and helpers, and if they reached out, there were those who would reach back. And maybe, just maybe, in that moment people on both sides of the street who saw and were touched by one another discovered the peace that Santa had offered.

Another beauty is that all of us who received his smile, his wave, and his gift were forced to look inward and ask questions:

"Am I at peace?"

"If not, why not?"

"And, how can I get from where I am to where I want to be?"

The simple truth is that I can never give away that which I do not possess. If I am to be a conduit of joy and peace to others, those qualities must first exist within my own being. "Peace, my man!" Santa said as he smiled in my direction. As I smiled back, a flood of unexpected questions came pouring in: "I am at peace in this setting in this moment, but am I at peace with life? With my world? With myself?" Joy, peace, and all other worthy virtues are within our reach. But there are things required of us in order to obtain them—openness, for example, and a re-evaluation of priorities, a deeper understanding of what things matter most, a restructuring of values, a commitment to focus more on sunlight than on shadows, as well as a rediscovery of the undeniable wisdom that we just get one shot at this thing called "life" and thus can ill afford to settle for a lesser form of living than we desire or deserve.

"Peace, my man!" he called to men at the cafés on Ocean Drive. "Peace, lovely lady!" to women carrying bags out of the boutiques. And the same greetings he shared with other men rising up from fitful sleep on park benches and with women looking for a bite of lunch someone else had thrown away. He treated us all the same, for apparently, he understood that down deep we are. We all share a sense of pain or longing. We all need to have smiles restored, as well as hope.

"Peace, my man!" "Peace, lovely lady!" "Peace!" I think the table server was correct. That man on South Beach really was Santa. When we find joy and peace and pass those things along to others, we can be Santa as well.

The Passenger On The Elevator

"Small is the gate and narrow the road that leads to life, and only a few find it."

(Matthew 7:14,

New International Version)

I was on my way to my office, a temporary space to be used while my permanent one was being renovated. I liked the temporary quarters and was in no hurry to evacuate them. Located on the tenth floor of a building soon to be taken down, it was a nice spot, roomy and light. My temporary area actually consisted of three rooms in a suite looking out on 29th Street. Through those windows I could see rooftop apartments with plants that were well-tended and green. I could see an outdoor restaurant, also on a roof, with young people eating, drinking, and flirting. I saw the photographer in his studio taking pictures of models to sell to magazines. I saw the street vendors selling their trinkets to tourists. So, I was almost always eager and enthusiastic when I boarded the elevator because I was headed to a good space to do work that I enjoy.

That particular morning when I stepped onto the elevator, I noticed a young woman who was already inside. She was well dressed, tall, thirty years old at the most. I asked what seemed a reasonable question, given that I was going to the top floor and no buttons had yet been pushed. "Where are you going?"

Without lifting her eyes to meet mine, she answered, "I don't know. It doesn't matter." That is an appropriate response to many questions, I suppose, but not ordinarily to the one I had posed.

Who enters an elevator without knowing or caring what floor number to push? Don't you step onto an elevator because you are going somewhere specific? You have a destination in mind, and this wooden box suspended on cables will get you there. Push the right button, get off at the right floor. But this young lady implied that she had no destination in mind and no interest in naming one. She had entered the elevator before I did and apparently had just stood there, pushing no button at all.

"Where are you going?"

"I don't know. It doesn't matter."

It was a Cheshire Cat moment, like the one when he advised Alice that if you don't care where you're going, then any road will get you there. I'm not comfortable with that. The woman on the elevator had not invited me into a conversation about any of that, so I didn't venture there... at least, not verbally. But mentally, I responded, "Oh yes, it does matter where you are going. It matters very much." Having a destination in mind establishes parameters for life. The destination or goal dictates what roads we take in order to arrive.

If my dream is to be a professional athlete, then part of the daily discipline I must follow is strenuous exercise under the tutelage of a trainer. I run. I work out with weights. But, it is about more than just exercise. It is also about diet. Therefore, again under the guidance of a nutritionist, I eat the right foods at the right times in the right amounts. But, it is about more than just diet. It is also about learning. Hence, I listen carefully to the advice of coaches whose business it is to help me learn the sport and how to succeed at it. They assist me in identifying my unique talents and where they best fit into that particular sport. If I am on a football team, and if I weigh 340 pounds and am as strong as a

Clydesdale, a good coach will not train me to be a running back, even if that is what I desire to do. He knows I am better suited to play the line, opening holes for smaller, quicker people who will run with the ball. In short, if my goal is to be a professional athlete, I do not simply walk onto a field or court or track and compete. The bulk of my life is spent on a journey of conditioning, training, and learning so that I can reach my desired destination.

The same is true of virtually any profession. If one's goal is to be an attorney, she or he goes to law school, studies and learns, then takes the bar exam and works under the guidance of seasoned practitioners. If one's goal is to be clergy, the person goes to seminary to study and learn, consequently taking strenuous exams for ordination and then often serves on a staff as an associate before becoming the lead pastor of a church. If one's goal is to be a physician, they go to med school for their education, then probably serve as an intern and later as a resident and after passing state certification, open their own practice or join a hospital. Pick a profession, and the process is similar. Where we wish to go in life, to a great extent, determines how we live and function day to day. There are specific roads that take us to specific places, and unless they are faithfully followed, we are little more than a hamster in a meaningless maze.

It matters how we choose to get to where we want to go. Not just any road will do. If I desire to go to California, I better take a highway headed west. If I desire to be a writer, I better read and study the works of successful writers. I also need to work with well-trained professors of literature and, of course, practice the craft. Write rough drafts and edit them, often throwing them away and beginning the process all over again. If I wish to be a chef, I do not just throw random items and spices into a pot, assuming that a soufflé will magically emerge. Instead, I choose the proper ingredients and blend them according to a specific recipe. I add flavors at the right times in the process and bake it all for a certain number of minutes in an oven set at an exact temperature.

Just so, if I want to find a meaningful life, there are steps I need to take. I have to come to a reasonable understanding of self. That is not an understanding that should be fashioned by the negative opinions of others, the demeaning voices we may have heard somewhere along the line. They cannot be allowed to form who we will become in life. If you had parents or teachers who made you feel unworthy or unable, as an adult you need to erase their tapes that too often play in your head. "You can't do this," or "You'll never accomplish that," have to be abandoned and replaced with a stronger voice, your own voice, telling you that the size of your achievements will be limited only by the size of your imagination.

If I want to find a meaningful life, I need to develop a reasonable worldview. I need to see people neither as dashing knights who will rescue nor as potential enemies who will harm. They are simply people, no more, no less. They may have authority over us (e.g., at work), but they do not own our emotions. They cannot dictate whether or not we will see the world in a hopeful, positive way. If they are depressed or despondent, though I care, I will not take on their negativity. It belongs to them, just as my outlook belongs to me.

I will see the world populated by people who are on a journey, just as I am. Their religions and politics may differ from my own, but that is fine, too. We do not have to believe all things together in order to simply be together, and to do so in a peaceful, productive way. "Live and let live" (as long as it does not lead to a mindset that is self-absorbed or lacking in compassion) is not an entirely bad philosophy.

It does matter where I am going. And it matters deeply how I choose to get there. In our building, that young woman was pretty safe. But out there in the world, if you don't have some idea of where you want to go, then any floor will do. Unfortunately, when you step off on some floors in life, you can find yourself in pretty scary places.

I pushed my button and said, as cheerfully as I knew how, "Well, you can accompany me to the tenth floor." She responded by saying, "Why are you talking to me? Leave me alone!"

That, I thought, was another strange response. It did not sound so much like rudeness as self-defense. I immediately wondered what frightening memory I represented. There she was, alone in a closed and small space with a man she did not know. A man twice her age. A man who was visibly "taking charge" of the moment. What childhood memories did that brief encounter call up for her? What emotional buttons were pushed? What fears rushed to the surface that I had no way of knowing about or understanding? Sometimes, when people respond to us in ways that seem inappropriate or hard to interpret, it actually may have little or nothing at all to do with us. Our moment in the elevator reminded me of that.

Maybe I had simply put her in an embarrassing situation. On the fourth and fifth floors of our building was a counseling center. When I stepped onto the elevator, she had her cell phone in hand, typing in digits and looking at the screen. Possibly she had found the right building for the center but was having difficulty finding the precise floor. And just as possible, she did not want to announce to a perfect stranger that she was there in need of therapy. An obvious response to such fears, of course, would have been, "Who couldn't use a trained listener?" Whose life would not benefit if from time to time we shared our dreams, our fears, our guilt, our grief, our sense of self, our insecurities, our desires with someone who can help us interpret what all that means? Why would anyone any longer associate that with weakness, embarrassment or shame, any more than one would be embarrassed to seek the assistance of a dentist or internist? Her response, defensive and adversarial, made me wonder if, indeed, she was not in search of someone on the fourth or fifth floors.

When the bell sounded for Number Ten, I exited. Before the elevator door closed, I said to her, "All of us who work in this building are here to help people—anyone at any time. It's what we do. Don't forget where we are in case you ever need us." Still she did not look up from her phone, but as the doors closed, I heard her whisper a single word. "Thanks." I hope she found what she was looking for that day. And, in a greater sense, I hope she finds a sense of destination that adds meaning to her life every day.

As I reflect on that elevator ride, three takeaways come to mind.

[1] Choosing the best roads always takes us to the best places.

How we craft the journey of life determines what destination we will arrive at, so it really matters which buttons we push in life's elevator.

[2] Our history impacts our present, but it does not have to shape our future.

Though an individual cannot change what was done for or to that person in years gone by, we can decide not to let a negative influence determine what comes next. Often, that is best done by seeking the advice of a trained listener who can teach us to throw off yesterday's shackles and be liberated for tomorrow.

[3] There is no shame in seeking the counsel of that trained listener.

Those professionals are skilled in helping us see and move through the past to a future unshackled by yesterday's pains or abuses. "When we learn from rather than run from our past, it can actually become a powerful part of our healing story." (Becca Stevens, *Love Heals*, Nashville: Thomas Nelson Publishers, 2017, p. 148) Good therapists facilitate that in unique and transformative ways.

There is a life we desire and deserve. Sometimes, we need someone else to show us what buttons to push on the elevator. Once we have arrived at our desired destination, we just may find ourselves equipped to assist someone else who is making a similar voyage.

Good Samaritans

"'Which of these three do you think was a neighbor to the man who fell into the hands of robbers?'

The expert in the law replied, 'The one who had mercy on him.'

Jesus told him, 'Go and do likewise.'"

(Luke 10:36-37,

New International Version)

I had not been a resident of New York City long when I had to attend a meeting at a huge square building located on Riverside Drive, across the street from several other huge square buildings that look almost exactly the same.

Crawling out of the back seat of a taxi, I found myself standing on a street corner surrounded by those nondescript, similar-looking edifices. No signs pointed me in the right direction. There was no marquis announcing which building was which. As I stood there considering my options (unsure of which door to try first), a couple approached me. They paused momentarily as if studying me, much as I was studying the structures before me. In a moment, the woman spoke: "You look lost. What are you looking for, and how can we help?"

It was not the first time I had that experience during my initial months in the city. Only two weeks earlier I had been on the Upper East Side to attend a meeting which, as it turned out, was on the Upper West Side. As I was walking up a street in Harlem, an older gentleman approached me and asked, "May I help you find whatever you're looking for?" When I explained where I needed to be, he shook his head, chuckled (not at me, but with me at my predicament), and said, "Every island has two sides. You picked the wrong one." He then graciously took all the time I needed to answer all the questions I had, ultimately getting me to where I needed to go. On yet another occasion I stood on Park Avenue outside the entrance to the 33rd Street subway, so new to the city and its underground transit system that I was unsure if that particular train would take me uptown or downtown. A woman approached. Small in stature, on that dreadfully cold morning, she was wrapped in so huge a coat and accompanying tam that she looked very much like a female version of Charlie Brown dressed for winter by his overprotective mom. "Pardon me," she said, "but you look like you could use some directions." I nodded. She replied, "Okay, tell me where you need to go, and I'll tell you how to get there."

I explained my newness in her city and my uncertainty about making the right subway connection. She smiled and inquired where I was going. I supplied an address, to which she answered, "Do you have a cell phone?" Assuring her I did, she went on, "Take it out, and write down these directions. You'll have to take this train for a few stops and then change to another. It can be confusing until you get the hang of it." Patiently she gave me directions, pausing for me to type them into the cell phone at a slow hunt-and-peck pace.

When at last I had the directions in print, like a schoolteacher addressing a third-grader, she said, "Now, read them back to me." I complied. With a smile larger than life, she exclaimed, "Good! You've got it. Now you're not lost anymore."

I often tell friends from below the Mason-Dixon line that what they call "Southern hospitality" extends much further north than they sometimes imagine. From the very beginning of my years in that large, rapid-paced metropolis, I ran across person after person who was willing to slow down and patiently offer assistance. "Tell me where you need to go, and I'll tell you how to get there."

Headlines convey some truth, but they do not convey the whole truth. I suspect not many papers would be sold if the front-page stories were about urban angels who are patient with strangers. But, headlines or not, those stories exist and are told in real life and in real time every single day. Unless one simply fails to pay attention, it is impossible not to notice takeaways from many of our chance encounters.

[1] *Acts of mercy are a large part of the fabric with which our society is woven.*

In sermons, speeches and blogs, I often talk about creating "a culture of kindness." One of the foundations on which such a culture would be built is simple courtesy. Courtesy does not require agreeing with the other person on every issue. It certainly does not require allowing one's self to be absorbed or abused by another. It simply means treating others with the same measure of respect and attention that we desire from them.

My mother taught me the value of verbal courtesy. "Please" and "Thank you" were non-negotiables. So were "Ma'am" and "Sir." Those seem such little things over against the major issues of the day, but how many tragedies born of anger might never have occurred if somewhere along the line the perpetrator had simply been treated courteously and respectfully? If we sow kindness in others, more often than not we will reap kindness from them. Even chance encounters become seeds that blossom in circles wider than we ever dared to dream or imagine. We may never see it happen, but that does not mean it will not occur.

One of the determining factors in how I deal with table servers in restaurants is the memory of a conversation I had some time ago with the wife of a table server. She said she could tell when he had experienced graciousness and generosity from a client (or clients) by the way he acted when his shift was over. "I hear him whistling when he walks through the door," she said, "or I feel a warm hug and kiss on the cheek, and I know someone has given him a generous tip or a healthy compliment. But there are other nights," she continued, "when he comes home sullen or angry. A patron has been demeaning or hateful to him. They refused to tip or complained about him to his supervisor. And the anger they stir up in him, he brings home to me." I've never forgotten that conversation. I keep it in mind when I interact with persons in public jobs. I never know if some small act on my part might have serious consequences later on for someone else. It is a fact that how I treat you will determine how you treat him, which will determine how he treats her, and on and on it goes. So if I set something in motion, I need to make certain it is the right something. Simple courtesy sets the right something in motion.

An additional takeaway should not be missed.

[2] *It is an undeniable fact that everyone needs help with something in some way.*

None of us is omnipotent. One of the most gifted public speakers I know (who does extraordinarily well on the motivational circuit) has to have his wife put on his socks and shoes for him every morning. No one would suspect that when they see him marching back-and-forth on a stage, captivating his audience and owning that space. But, he suffers from spinal arthritis in the lower back. Most mornings he has to move about slowly for a while in order to become limber enough to have the fluid movement we all assume is his 24/7. When he gets out of bed each day, he simply cannot bend over sufficiently to put on socks and shoes. However in control of things he may appear, he is dependent on someone else's kindness to do for him what to many is a genuinely simple task. The point is that we all need something we cannot provide to ourselves. No one is so powerful that he or she is not in some way dependent on the kindnesses of others. When we figure that out, three important things occur. (1) We become less hesitant about asking for assistance. It is not a sign of weakness. It is a sign of humanness. (2) We become more keenly aware of those wonderful moments when people have offered kindness to us, even moments when it was offered before we asked. And, (3) If we are touched by that, we become more willing to extend a helping hand to others, whether or not it is requested. By giving life away, we often find it.

There really is a culture of kindness in the world. It doesn't often make the headlines, but it does make life livable in the most essential ways. We can be citizens of that culture. All that's required is to be aware and to be willing…

aware of the Good Samaritans who often step forward to help us find our way, and *willing* to step forward for others who for a moment need assistance along their way. That couple on Riverside Drive belongs to the culture of kindness. So does the older, very patient gentleman in Harlem. So does the school teacher-ish woman at the Park Avenue subway. With care and concern, they approached a stranger and spoke: "You look lost. What are you looking for, and how can we help?" They offered me kindness and, thus, inspired me to pass it along. As W.H. Auden observed: "If there when grace dances, I should dance." (*Collected Poems*, London: Vintage Press, 1991)

A Maître d' In Charleston

"For where your treasure is, there will your heart be also."

(Matthew 6:21,

New International Version)

Charles Kuralt traveled across America for a living, reporting on who he met and what he observed. Via his books and his television presence, many of us were given the chance to travel with him to places we otherwise would never be or see. He wrote once that if you could visit twelve places in the U.S., one should be Charleston, South Carolina, in spring when the flowers are blooming (from *Charles Kuralt's America*, NY: NY, Knopf Doubleday Publishing, 1996). I think he was onto something. I have never resided in Charleston, but I have visited on numerous occasions. The city is a somewhat smaller and more slowly paced version of New

Orleans. It rests on the Atlantic, has cobblestone streets and horse-drawn carriages, and affords opportunities for world-class music, culture, shopping, tranquility, beauty, and cuisine. As a lifelong fan of food, that latter quality (cuisine) attracts me to places like that gentle southern seaside community.

On a warm spring evening, my wife and I joined two other couples to dine in a restaurant in Charleston's historic section. It was attached to a well-known hotel. The maître d' seated us in an enclosed courtyard, handed us beautifully bound leather menus and wine lists, and welcomed us courteously to his establishment.

"Are you visiting in our city?" he asked.

We replied that two of the three couples were.

"So, where do you live?" he continued, to which we responded, "We out-of-towners are from New York City."

"New York City!" the maître d' said with a smile and a polite note of approval. "Some of our chefs were trained there. I used to live there myself, but only for a short period of time. Great place." We thanked him, agreed that it is a great place, and confirmed that we loved being residents of the Big Apple.

"You have some of the best food in the world in New York City," he continued.

"I can't imagine any better," I responded.

He looked at me, still smiling but with an unmistakable seriousness in his eyes, and answered, "Yes, you have some fine food in New York City. But, just wait. You haven't tasted ours yet!"

I don't recall what we ate that night. But I do recall thinking as we paid our bill that the maître d' delivered on his promise. As I had said of our cuisine back home, so did I find myself saying of our meal that night: "I can't imagine any better."

Reflecting on that evening, and especially on that man who loved his city and the quality of its food, three takeaways come to mind.

[1] Be proud of what you have.

The maître d' in Charleston complimented what others brought to the table (literally), but he was equally proud of what he had to offer. The fact that our gifts or skills are different from someone else's does not make ours (or theirs) inferior. "Different from" by no means equals "lesser than."

A TV sportscaster on a network football game commented that, "Every team rises or falls on the shoulders of its quarterback." Admittedly, QB is a key position. The better he is, the stronger your team is likely to be. And yet, how could that person perform his job without an offensive lineman who protect him from a pass rush? Without the big guys up front doing their jobs, he would never have the time to throw a single pass before being flat on his back. So, whose role is more important? The answer appears to be that each role is significant in its own unique way.

Some people enjoy small, private cruise boats with a dozen friends sailing the Mediterranean. Others take pleasure in large cruise liners with thousands of people sailing the Caribbean, while there are some who would simply be having fun on a bass boat with a grandkid on a small lake. All are forms of boating as a leisure activity. Each is significantly different from the others. None is necessarily superior or inferior. The old adage "Whatever floats your boat" more than applies. If you enjoy it, if it brings you pleasure, then it is at the pinnacle of your own personal hill. Duke Ellington was correct in his answer to the question, "What is good music?" He replied, "Whatever is good to you."

As a teen, I would sometimes come home bragging after being with friends who possessed things I envied. My father, a wise and grounded person, was always able to put life back into perspective for me in those moments.

"Dad, you should see his car. It's sleek and fast and new!"

"Son," he consistently answered, "a car has one purpose—to get you from Point A to Point B. If his or yours serves that purpose, then it's a good car."

Or, I would return to our very normal home from time with a friend who lived in, what seemed to me, a mansion and say, "Wow, Dad! Their house is huge."

Again, he had a standard reply (and an accurate one): "Son, you can only live in one room at a time."

Looking back, I understand now that I had a car that would safely transport me where I needed to go. And, I had a home with secure shelter, warmth, food, and unlimited love. What I had was of no lesser value than that of anyone else. Different, yes. Less, no. As an old adage puts it: *The secret to having what you want is learning to want what you have.*

To find happiness in life requires taking stock of what we have in our lives (health, friends, family members, material possessions, freedom, etc.) and not contrasting our ledgers to the next person's. Become aware of what you have and be grateful. Countless others probably look at you with envy. The maître d' didn't worry about foods served in New York City. He was happy with the delicacies he had to offer up in Charleston.

[2] *Be proud of where you are.*

I loved our time in NYC. I love our current time in NC. The Maitre' D loved Charleston. Some of my dear friends live in small communities in the Appalachian Mountains, others in walking distance of the Atlantic Ocean, others in Midwest farm communities, and still others in large metropolitan areas on the West Coast. Many of them have said to me with unequivocal conviction, "I live in the best place on earth!" Each of them is correct. Where they have chosen to live, the place they love and call "home," is the best place for them. Those residences are not in competition with one another. Each provides experiences that are unique. Each is a source of deep happiness for people who choose to see the beauties that exist there. Each is, therefore, a wellspring both of personal satisfaction and of pride to the residents whose hearts and lives are invested there.

I grew up in a small town in central North Carolina. When I was a child, the population of my hometown was about 10,000. We had one small hospital with three surgeons. There was one high school, one movie theater with a single screen, two men's clothing stores, two women's clothing stores, two department stores, and two dime stores. On the south end of our town's main drag was a grocery store. On the north end was another. A number of curb markets stayed open late enough to allow people to get bread or milk once the grocery stores had closed.

In my adult life to this point, I have lived in numerous large cities with every amenity imaginable available in abundance. For about a decade, I lived in a city of eight million people that sold anything and everything one can purchase 24/7. And yet, as a child in that small southern town, I was not aware of being without the things that brought quality to life. We lived in a modest but nice house. I was clothed, fed, and protected. In my neighborhood were seven of us guys approximately the same age. Though I had neither brothers or sisters, those friends felt like family in a genuine *Our Gang* sort of way.

My schools taught me the three Rs (Reading, 'Riting, and 'Rithmetic) plus character and kindness. We went to a traditional church where the music was good and the pastor knew our names and stories. I played Little League baseball and participated in Scouts. I was in and out of our little hospital on several occasions and always received appropriate treatment that made me well. We had a TV that was connected to an antenna on the roof and had to be manually turned to enhance the reception of the four channels we received. I didn't anticipate a day with cable and hundreds of channels, but instead was perfectly satisfied with the entertainment our four channels provided. We had a rotary phone and had never heard of laptops or iPads. Nonetheless, I communicated with whomever I needed to as effectively (and perhaps even more personally) than I do now via emails. My car was a stick shift before that became cool.

My hometown was not a hub of excitement. No nightclubs. No professional sports teams. No theme parks or casinos. But it was filled with good people and fresh green spaces to explore and a sense of community that is sometimes specific to smaller towns and an adventurous imagination of what other faraway places might be like. Most of all, it was filled with love from family and friends. It was a good and safe place, and I relished growing up there. I'm thankful I had that opportunity and would not trade it. I was proud of where I was. Looking back, even though I haven't lived there in many years, I'm still proud. And thankful.

Create your own litany of good qualities about wherever you are at this moment. If it is *home* to you, permanently or just for a season, name the blessings associated with being there. For there are blessings wherever we happen to be if we just pay attention. The maître d' complimented New York. But he was proud of Charleston.

[3] *Be proud of who you are.*

A man I know from Dallas, Texas, spent a week at a corporate meeting in Chicago. He had been flown in as a consultant and, thus, made several presentations over the course of the week. Toward the end of the event, he sat and chatted one evening with several participants at a closing banquet. Though complimentary of what he had done, the group concurred that they were captivated by how he spoke.

"You sound like a cowboy," one of them said. "We're just fascinated by your accent."

He answered, "That's funny. All week I have been listening to you and thinking I am the only person at this meeting who doesn't have an accent!"

He was not willing to be put down, even in jest. His essential self, he was saying, was just as valid as anyone else's. When relating that story, he concluded, "You don't have to be like somebody else in order to be real." I understood that.

When I first arrived in NYC after living in the South since birth, my regional accent was unmistakable. Trying to prove I was a quick study of her large city, early on in my tenure there, I said to a New Yorker, "I understand they speak 168 different languages right here in these five boroughs."

Immediately she answered, "169 now!" It was funny. In a way, it was true. And it was okay. If all those from varying nations of origin could speak proudly with their native tongues, so could I. The man from Dallas was correct. You don't have to be like somebody else in order to be real. In fact, trying to be like somebody else makes authenticity impossible.

A nun I know leads weekend *Self-Understanding Retreats* all across the country. She begins each weekend by asking the participants to make a brief statement beginning with the words, "Here's what is beautiful about me..." Initially, as one might expect, most people are highly uncomfortable doing so. Many try to make jokes, most of them self-deprecating. But, she refuses to allow that.

"No," she will respond. "That's not acceptable. There is so much good about you. Tell us at least one good thing about yourself that comes to mind." Then she forces them to start over, saying, "Here's what is beautiful about me..." As those who attend her events are led session-by-session into deeper understanding of their gifts, skills, and potential, it becomes easier for them to complete that statement (which they are required to do at the close of each session). "By our last night together," she laughs, "sometimes I have to interrupt and remind some of them that we need to allow someone else a chance to talk, too."

That nun leads her students on a remarkably important journey—the journey to understanding that you are a person of dignity and worth, that no one else is superior to you (nor you to them), that others are merely different. If we do not like ourselves, we will not like others. If we do not respect ourselves, we will not know how to respect others. But, healthy self-love equips us to love other people as they are. Be proud of who you are. There's no one else like you. You are the only you there is. That's a special piece of knowledge to be embraced and celebrated.

"You have some fine food in New York City," the maître d' commented. "But, just wait. You haven't tasted ours yet!"

Dizzy Dean used to say, "It ain't bragging if you can back it up," and that Charleston restaurant more than delivered on what had been promised.

Be proud of what you have.

Be proud of where you are.

Be proud of who you are.

And whenever possible, help others to discover those secrets to finding a life that brings joy and fulfillment.

I Don't Want To Be Here

"Then Saul dressed David in his own tunic. He put a coat of armor on him and a bronze helmet on his head. David fastened on his sword over the tunic and tried walking around, because he was not used to them. 'I cannot go in these,' he said to Saul, 'because I am not used to them.' So he took them off. Then he took his staff in his hand, chose five smooth stones from the stream, put them in the pouch of his shepherd's bag and, with his sling in his hand, approached the Philistine."

(I Samuel 17:38-40,

New International Version)

Following an afternoon class I taught at High Point University, I was straightening up the room for the next professor—erasing the white board, putting chairs back in place, closing windows that had been cracked open, and making certain that the AV equipment for PowerPoint presentations was in "Start" mode.

As I tended to those tasks, a young female student walked in fifteen minutes early for her class. She made her way to a desk at the rear of the room and was in the process of opening her backpack while I was in the process of closing my briefcase to walk out. I didn't know her but felt compelled to be polite.

"Hi!" I said. "I hope your class will be a good one."

As I turned toward the door, she answered: "I don't want to be here." What an interesting response to a perfunctory remark, especially coming from a perfect stranger. It also seemed like a moment that demanded I say something in return.

"Well," it's early in the semester," I offered. "New classes always seem a bit strange at this point. You'll find your rhythm."

"It's not that I don't want to be in this particular class," she continued. "I don't want to be in any class. I don't want to be in college at all."

Returning a couple of paces from the door, I faced her and asked, "Where do you want to be?"

"In a kitchen," she replied. "Or, if in school, then in a culinary school. I want to cook. It's all I've ever wanted to do. Right now I should be preparing meals and plating them for hungry folks who I'm about to make happy. Instead I'm here, doing just the opposite of that."

"So, why are you here instead of in a kitchen somewhere?"

"Because everyone else wants me to be."

"Explain."

"My grandmother came to this university when it was just a small college. She always wanted me to get a degree from here like she did. My parents wanted me to go to college and began saving for that from the day I was born. My teachers in high school encouraged me to go to college. All my friends just assumed that's what I would do. Whenever I told any of them that I wanted to cook, they laughed it off. They called it 'a hobby,' something I could do on weekends for fun or relaxation. So, here I am because they want me to be."

I wasn't quite sure how to respond to a stranger who had not asked for advice. She had instead just vented frustrations. I looked at her without speaking. She gazed down at the contents of her backpack, which she had randomly placed atop her desk. After a few seconds her eyes rose and once more met mine. She said with notes both of defiance and confidence: "I feel like I'm chasing everyone's dream except my own. But you watch. Things are going to change. One day you're going to turn on the Food Network, and you'll be looking at me!" By then other students were entering the room, and our exchange would no longer have remained confidential.

"You know where I am if you want to continue this chat," I said. She nodded and looked away. We never talked again.

"I feel like I'm chasing everyone's dream except my own." In defense of those who had encouraged her to pursue higher education, my guess is that they cared deeply about that young woman. They wanted the best for her. They desired that she position herself for a future with promise and potential. Probably none of them intended to force an artificial dream upon her. Rather, I suspect, they wanted to make sure that she became adequately prepared to open every attractive professional door possible. And yet, their well-intended guidance failed to appreciate her deepest longings and her dearest joys. Likewise, they minimized the sacred nature of her dream. To her, it was a calling. To them, it was at best only "a hobby."

The first takeaway as I remember that encounter is that:

[1] *We must assess our own lives.*

No one else fully understands what it means to be you. Nor is that possible for them since they do not live in your skin. No one else knows exactly what your frustrations feel like, nor do they know what your joys feel like, just as you cannot know theirs. No one else can say, "This is what makes you happy," unless you have told them it does.

That student knew her source of joy precisely because it was *her* source. Hopefully she respected the choices made by her grandmother, parents, teachers, and friends. She simply articulated a need for them to reciprocate vis-à-vis her choices.

Assess what you do well. Evaluate what brings delight to your life. Then if you can find a way to marry those two things, you will have found your own unique road to fulfillment.

The second takeaway is that:

[2] *You can never be happy chasing someone else's dream.*

To be sure, it is always wise to listen to the advice of others. We should take their counsel seriously. If they are people who have lived a sufficient number of years, we are well advised to value their experience and wisdom. And, we should be aware that most of the time people encourage us because they love us and want what's best for us. And yet, having listened, pondered, and appreciated, when crunch time comes we are the only ones who can construct our own dreams.

Ralph Waldo Emerson reminded us that, "Envy is ignorance, and imitation is suicide." (from his essay *Self Reliance*) Whereas that student did not envy others who had followed different paths, she did feel pressured to imitate their decisions. Her grandmother desired that she walk in her footsteps at the same university she had attended. Her parents, teachers, and friends assumed there was only one path to be followed—the same her mom and dad had traveled and her friends were about to travel. She should fall in stride and do likewise.

Wisely, the student had begun to discern something of indisputable importance: "I feel like I'm chasing everyone's dream except my own." Life is a rapid journey. In its course, we will experience countless flights of fancy. Amid those, however, will be a handful of legitimate dreams. They are distinctively personal. They are, also, doorways to potential happiness in the myriad seasons of life. Don't let an authentic dream go unexamined. Neither let it be inordinately delayed. Often with the passage of time, windows of opportunity close and cannot be reopened. If you have a dream that is your own, pursue it. Either it will come true, or other things of value will be discovered simply in its pursuit. Either way, it is win/win.

A final takeaway is this:

[3] *Believe in your own gifts*.

"You watch… One day you're going to turn on the Food Network, and you'll be looking at me!" I wouldn't be at all surprised.

The list is long of famous individuals who were discouraged from chasing their dreams. Einstein, Darwin, Walt Disney, Oprah, Edison, Elvis, Lady Gaga, Lincoln, Lucille Ball, Van Gogh, Emily Dickinson, Rudyard Kipling. The litany goes on and on. Each one, however, believed in his or her abilities and persevered (to all of our good fortune). Your name can be on that list. So, I suspect, will be the name of a college student whose dream is to make hungry people happy.

To reiterate, the questions are: What can you do? And, what brings you joy? Those are the essential building blocks of a meaningful dream. Believing in its worth, and in your own, is the mortar that will transform those building blocks into a worthy structure.

Believing in yourself, in fact, includes believing in the value and legitimacy of *your* dream. Not someone else's. Yours! Disney wanted to draw cartoons. Lucille Ball wanted to act. Rudyard Kipling wanted to write. Each was advised to follow a different path. But each knew who they were and what they desired from life. They believed in themselves, and they believed in their dreams. Disney could probably have been a house painter. Kipling could probably have been a newspaper copy boy. Ball could probably have been a Hollywood makeup artist. But they had other dreams, and believed in them, and pursued them.

Similarly, no doubt there are dozens of things you can do with your life. From butcher to baker to candlestick maker, you have options. But which of those options excites you? Which possesses the possibility of bringing joy? You've got to believe in the value of your dream and in its potential for making a difference (in the lives of others and in your own). If you're not excited about it, don't chase it. That is a road that will ultimately wind up in an unfulfilling place.

This principle, of course, applies to more than just careers. It also has dramatic emotional and relational implications. Consider just one, and then apply it however it works best in your own experience.

A friend became estranged from one of his children. In time, the abyss between them deepened. There were long gaps of silence with no communication at all. The only breaks were prescribed and predictable—a couple of hours on Thanksgiving, Christmas, and Father's Day, but nothing more. Eventually even those occasions were no longer observed. My friend continued making regular contact with his son, always it appeared to no avail. He would text but receive no response. He would leave voicemails but receive no return call. He would send gifts but receive no acknowledgements. He would extend invitations to meet for a meal but receive no reply. Friends and other family members advised him to let it go, to quit torturing himself. But my friend persisted. His refrain was always: "I love my son, whether or not he loves me. So I will keep trying to build a bridge as long as it takes. I want my child back." It was his dream. He believed in it and refused to let it go.

Several months ago, he reported to me that his son had at last replied to one of his invitations. They met for dinner. It was awkward, he confessed, but it was a first step. Then came another dinner. Then a third. Now they are communicating by texts with some regularity. Recently the son texted something rather mundane to his father, but he concluded it with four words that were extraordinarily important: "I love you, Dad." Sharing that news with me, my friend said, "Thank God I didn't give up on my dream for us!"

Believe in yourself. Believe in your dream. Without that, dreams never come true. "You watch," she said as the other students began to arrive for class. "Things are going to change. One day you're going to turn on the Food Network, and you'll be looking at me!" I'm betting she's right.

I Still Have A Future

The man from whom the demons had gone out begged to go with him, but Jesus sent him away, saying, "Return home and tell how much God has done for you." So the man went away and told all over town how much Jesus had done for him.

(Luke 8:38-39,

New International Version)

The train ride from the city was beautiful and tranquil, much unlike the destination that awaited me. We traveled up the Hudson. To the left, I saw the river, wide, peaceful, deep, and strong. Vacation homes and boat landings were sprinkled along the way. To the right, I saw the lovely, quaint, picturesque towns to which that river, over many years, had given birth. Westchester. Kingston. Numerous others. They have a charm all their own, born of their history. There was beauty on that ride, from whichever window you peered. The steady clack-clack of the wheels would have had a sedative effect on other days, but not on that one.

I was on my way to Ossining, another picturesque and lovely community. But my destination was neither picturesque nor lovely. My assignment was to speak at a Graduation Ceremony inside the walls of Sing Sing Prison. It's a famous place, a maximum security institution that has existed since 1826. Prior to 1972, 614 men and women were electrocuted there. Among the most famous executions were those of Julius and Ethel Rosenberg, convicted of being Russian spies during the Cold War.

There are about two thousand residents at Sing Sing now. In the past it housed those whom New York judges considered to be the most heinous of criminals. If, in the opinion of the bench, you were among "the worst of the worst," they assigned you to Sing Sing. Even still, it is populated by numerous individuals who were convicted of singularly serious crimes ranging from drug trafficking to murder, with all sorts of alarming wrongdoings in addition.

It is a surreal moment when you first arrive at the prison. There it stands, a fortress of correctional authority. It looks like what it is, large and imposing. How many others have driven up to those gates knowing that once inside, they would never step out again? For over six hundred of them, they knew they would face execution there. And yet, when you look past the building, you see the beautiful Hudson flowing by with gentle hills adorning it. What emotions must be stirred within those confined there when they look out barred windows and view autumn colors ablaze beyond their reach, or winter snow falling softly on the water, or boats sailing by with passengers smiling, singing, and sipping wine, free to come and go as they choose?

It was a strange moment for me, as well, observing it all as I stepped out of the taxi. My audience was within those walls. I didn't know the names of those awaiting me, but I knew they were people who had dreams of a future beyond those walls. They had labored in prison classrooms to create the possibility of tomorrows that would be dramatically different from their yesterdays. At last, their Graduation Day had arrived. Families, friends, and faculty were gathering in their honor. And though the setting was vastly different from what would soon be occurring forty miles south at Columbia or NYU, the students' hopes for fresh starts and new beginnings were the same.

There was an initial orientation that visitors go through, the registration, the words about security, and a walk through a labyrinth of halls with the sound of locked doors closing behind you. For all the times I have spoken in correctional facilities, the walking-in experience still brings a touch of nervousness. I've never experienced anything but graciousness and hospitality from those who live there. And yet, the words of caution and the sound of locking doors create a visceral effect on those of us who do not walk through those doors daily.

We emerged into a large dining hall. Chairs had been set up in two sections of ten or twelve rows each. Tables were on one side of the room, with prison residents already behind them to serve cookies, coffee, and tea to participants following the ceremony. Those of us representing the university put on our robes and academic regalia. Then the processional line was called to order. Behind us were eleven men not in robes, but in prison gray uniforms. They were the graduates, individuals who had completed degrees with hopes of creating new lives. All the folding chairs were occupied by guests who had come to celebrate with and for a loved one. In all likelihood, they were the same people who once sat in a courtroom and wept as officers led that loved one out in handcuffs. This day, however, they sat in a prison dining hall and smiled as officials led their loved ones in to receive diplomas.

With a loudspeaker playing *Pomp and Circumstance*, we entered in a formal line, those of us who were free later on to walk out and those others who would be led back to locked cells. But in that moment, all alike were smiling. As I spoke to them prior to the awarding of diplomas, I talked about dreams and opportunities and how, having become different, we are then equipped to make a difference. I talked about how our experiences from the past teach lessons that prepare us for the future. I did the best I knew how to be authentic, affirming, and encouraging.

After the ceremony, with a plate of cookies in one hand and a cup of coffee in the other, I heard a better speech than I had delivered. And a shorter one. And a more powerful one that included a personal note of hope beyond that which I had articulated. I was seated with one of the graduates, having no idea what crime he had committed that landed him in Sing Sing, how long he had been there, nor how much longer he would remain behind those walls. I simply knew that he was a man who possessed (or perhaps was possessed by) an irrepressible dream. He said, "I fell in with some bad folks and did some bad things as a young man. Where I grew up, that was more the rule than the exception. I got caught and am paying my dues for the things I did in the past. But I still have a future, and this diploma is a reminder of that!"

"I still have a future." He told me about his plans for that future. His desire, upon being paroled, was to return to the neighborhood where he grew up and there to spend his life trying to intervene with other young people who were wrestling with serious decisions that could have devastating consequences. "I want to give some of them a chance to take a different road than I did," he told me. "I'm not sure most folks from the outside can get through to them. But, I'm not an outsider. I'm an insider. They'll know I've been there and paid the price. So, they can learn from me before they end up in some place like this." That was his dream. As he said, the diploma in his hand symbolized that. It was a reminder that he still had a future and, also, could have a role in helping other people craft theirs.

"I still have a future." How do his words become our own, even when most of us are outsiders? We haven't lived the sort of life he has. We haven't fallen so far or suffered so much. We haven't had to lift ourselves up in so dramatic a fashion. And yet, we do share some common ground with that graduate in gray. We have a future and want it to be filled with meaning. How can we make that happen?

The inmate's spirit of determination (the same spirit I observed in every person receiving a diploma that day) says to us *[1] Your past should not dictate your future*. For many years, I was pastor of Marble Collegiate Church in New York City. Norman Vincent Peale served in the same capacity when he wrote *The Power of Positive Thinking* (NY, NY: Prentice-Hall, 1952). In that global best-seller, he observed that "it is always too early to give up." It truly is. Yes, our journeys at times seem long, difficult, and tiring. Sometimes, all of us feel that we are treading a hamster's wheel and not making any headway at all. Why keep trying? Why put in the effort when no results seem to appear? The answer is that our vision is limited to what was and what is. We cannot see what is to yet come or how close it may be to happening. We never really know what lies around the very next corner. For many, it is the realization of a long-held and pursued dream. But they can never find it if they quit the journey before that corner is turned. It is always too early to give up. "I still have a future."

So, *[2] Name your dream*. And don't set the bar too low. If you're going to dream, dream big. That inmate spoke to me of his dream of returning to a neighborhood plagued by crime, despair, and a plethora of wrong roads to choose from. There are gangs there, competing for the allegiance of young people who are vulnerable and easy targets. His is a huge dream. What can one man do against such significant forces? "I'm an insider," he said confidently. "They'll know I've been there and paid the price. So, they can learn from me before they end up in some place like this." A big dream? Yes. But it lived in a big heart, and that makes room for dreams to come true. He will not rescue every young person who lives where he lived. But it is beyond doubt that he will have a transformative impact on some of them. In turn, they will have positive impacts on others. They will become constructive rather than criminal.

Name your dream, and dare to dream big. The old adage is correct that if we aim for the stars and fall short, at least we will hit the moon. If, instead, we aim only for something simple and easily achievable, where's the dreaming in that? And where is the sense of accomplishment when it comes true? Name your dream.

[3] After naming the dream, then you begin to believe in it. If I dream of doing something worthwhile but doubt that I can make it happen, then I will not make it happen. The dream will become nothing more than a pipedream, a pleasant fantasy that has nothing to do with how my reality is shaped.

Daring to dream "big," of course, does not mean that we should dare to dream "irrationally." Dream of that which falls within your sphere of possibility.

When I was a youth, I was a good baseball player. I wasn't the best in the league, but I wasn't the worst, either. I was a skillful first baseman, one year making an all-star team because of those skills. I could stretch to make the catch. I could dig a wayward throw out of the dirt. I could stop a line drive that should have been a hit. At first base, I was dependable. And for a while as a youth, I was a pretty effective hitter. One season among the home runs I hit, three (including two in one game) were hit off a pitcher who later on wound up signing with the Cleveland Indians. I could hit. So, I dreamed of the day when I would walk onto the field at Yankee Stadium as their first baseman. Why not? If you're going to dream, dream big.

Then something unexpected occurred. I first experienced it from that very pitcher against whom I previously had enjoyed such success. We had reached an age when people began throwing curve balls. I could hit a fastball. That was easy. It comes in a straight line. There's no guesswork. If you keep your eye on the ball and make contact, you can launch a rocket over the wall. Curves are not like that. They dance. They fall like a marble off a flat table. They move away from you when you think they're coming in. They come in when you think they're moving away. The pitcher who later signed with Cleveland threw me three straight curve balls the first time I faced him after he had mastered that art. I never took the bat off my shoulder. I was mesmerized watching what the ball was doing and was completely aware that I couldn't hit it with a bat the size of a telephone pole. He struck me out on three pitches and just grinned at me when I walked away. The tables had turned. I knew walking back to the bench that if I ever made it to Yankee Stadium, it would only happen after purchasing a ticket. It was a dream I had to give up because I did not have the specific talents required to make it come true.

However, realizing I couldn't hit a curve ball did not make me stop dreaming. Instead it made me refine my dreams, crafting them vis-à-vis my abilities. What did I believe about myself? What things could I do that didn't require hitting a curveball? In my case, I could stand before a group of people and speak. I gain energy and joy from doing that. Thus I decided that by doing what I love, perhaps I could help others find energy and joy, as well. In short, I simply changed my dream to one that I had the gifts to achieve. After taking that step, I dreamt big. I started imagining how I could make the most of my abilities to benefit the most people. And, I believed in the dream itself—that it was a good one, and I could attain it. Don't give up dreaming because your skill set doesn't match your aspirations. Instead, aspire to something you have the gifts to achieve or acquire. Then dare to dream big and to believe in your dream.

[4] Having named the dream, and believing that you can achieve it, at last you pursue it. "I still have a future," the resident of Sing Sing said to me behind barred windows. The future he envisioned was beyond the walls of that building. He named his dream—to return to his old neighborhood and make a difference. He dreamed big—to become an intervening agent of change that would redirect young lives. He believed in the dream—both in its moral value and in his ability to make it come true. And he

took action to do whatever was required to turn the dream into reality—starting with completing an academic degree that would one day position him to be hired and deployed by a professional agency that had a dream similar to his own.

It is true that a journey of a thousand miles begins with a single step. But, it does not conclude there. It requires step after step in pursuit of what seems like a distant goal. With each step, the goal becomes nearer and clearer. If your dream lifts you, then let the pursuit of it propel you into a new future.

I'm not sure where the man who chatted with me that night is now, his hard-earned degree in hand. But wherever he is, I know he's determined to chase his dream and make it come true. You see, he still has a future.

The Puppies On
Forty-Ninth Street

"I have other sheep that are not from this fold."

(John 10:16,

Tree of Life Version)

Walking the dogs was never my favorite duty while living in NYC. It wasn't the walking I disliked, or the dogs, but rather the picking up after them. But, that's part of life in a city where there's far more asphalt than grass. Add a little rain to the experience, and it fell even further down my list of preferred activities.

It was rainy on the morning after Halloween. Our two King Charles Cavalier Spaniels seemed undeterred by that while gleefully sniffing for parcels of candy the preceding night's trick-or-treaters had dropped on the sidewalk. As I turned to walk east on 49th

Street, we encountered a woman walking west with her Poodle. Her dog seemed just as enthusiastic about a hunt for Halloween leftovers as did my own. However, upon spotting each other, the three dogs momentarily abandoned the search for food in favor of a time of frenetic tail-wagging, nose-rubbing, and impromptu fellowship.

Our dogs had never met before. I have no idea if they possess some internal radar alerting them whether or not another canine is friendly. They just seemed to assume the best and met in a huddle of blissful newfound friendship while the other owner and I awkwardly tried to find something to say about dogs, weather, Halloween, etc.

Standing a few steps away, observing it all, was a man who worked in a nearby building. He was obviously a dog lover, as he watched the animals with a smile both wide and infectious. After taking it all in for maybe a full minute, he turned to the woman and me and spoke.

The lady with the Poodle was a native New Yorker. I was a transplant from the south. The man watching with the big smile had moved to our city from Mexico. Neither of us looks or sounds the same.

"Dogs get it, don't they? Look at them, tails going a mile a minute. They are different breeds, have different colored coats, and sound different when they bark. But they get it. Somehow they know that they're all just dogs, and they are meant to be together."

The Poodle owner and I nodded and mumbled something in reply, whereupon the woman summoned her dog and resumed her westward journey. I did the same, leading my two pups east of 1st Avenue toward the street where we lived. As I walked away, the doorman, still smiling broadly, said it again: "Dogs get it!"

Funny how we refer to pets as "lower life forms" while we are the ones working in labs to create missile launchers and chemical weapons or walking around in camouflage outfits, toting AK-15s and pretending to be Rambo. Historically, we are the ones who never seem to "get it."

When I was an elementary school child in the South, I had a buddy who lived two streets over. We loved to meet in the afternoons and play the games that children play in the fascinating world of make-believe. Our favorites, as I recall, were cops-and-robbers (we both loved the comics section of the news, our hero being Dick Tracy) and "Let's Pretend" (in which we would imagine becoming heroes on our own in some fantasy future).

We built a labyrinth once. New neighbors had moved into a house nearby. They left dozens of packing boxes by the curb to be picked up by waste management. Instead, they were picked up by my friend and myself. A couple of rolls of tape transformed those boxes into a long tube with twists and turns. We could make it become anything we desired simply by saying, "Let's pretend." "Let's pretend it's an underground tunnel and we are soldiers sneaking up on enemy headquarters." "Let's pretend it's the opening to a cave where Blackbeard the Pirate hid his treasures." "Let's pretend it's an escape route from someplace where the bad guys held us captive, but we dug this out while they were sleeping." The possibilities were endless.

Sometimes, he would bring his baseball glove to my place, and we would become pitcher and catcher in the seventh game of the World Series. Often I would take my football to his house, and we would be opponents in the Orange Bowl. We especially loved that game if it had recently rained or snowed. What's more fun for a kid than being tackled in the mud? (Of course, what's less fun for the parent at home who does the laundry?)

Our moms made sure we did our homework before we met in the afternoons. First things first, you know. They also made sure we did it correctly. So we would labor to be (a) quick and (b) accurate. He and I didn't want to waste valuable cops-and-robbers or "Let's pretend" time doing school work after we had spent the whole day doing the same work inside a school. When we met, frequently one of us would have a tale to tell about something that had happened that day in the classroom or on the playground. Some of the stories were scary. Others were funny. Most were exaggerated (a variation of "Let's pretend"). But, the tale was always new to the child who heard it. Never once had both of us seen the same thing occur in exactly the same way. That was because my friend and I were not allowed to attend the same school. He was black, and I was white. In that hard-to-imagine era, schools were segregated. So were public bathrooms. So were public water fountains. So were churches. Even if we went together to see the same Saturday matinee at the theater, we had to meet afterward to discuss it because he could only be seated in the balcony, and I could only be seated downstairs. When we were able to be together, he and I were like puppies meeting on 49th Street, celebrating friendship without knowing we were different.

We didn't know that Poodles and Spaniels are two breeds apart. We thought we were both just puppies, and that brought us together.

A man I knew years ago returned home from his first trip to The Holy Land. While there, he visited a small community jointly populated by Israelis and Palestinians. In that community, he and his guide watched a group of children playing soccer on a dirt street. The children ran and laughed together, enjoying the sport they loved and the friends who played it with them. My friend reported that his guide watched the children silently for a moment, then turned to him and said, "Some of those children are Muslim. Others are Christian. Some are Jewish. Look at them having fun together just being children, nothing more, nothing less. You know the sad thing?" he said to my friend. "The sad thing," he continued, "is that they will not know they are supposed to hate one another until adults teach them to." On that day, on that street, playing that game, they were just "puppies." They "got it," but would soon have "it" stolen from them.

Not all that many years ago, those were our world's standards and stories. Segregation based on the color of one's skin. Glass ceilings and unfair wages based on one's gender. Prejudice toward people, jokes about people, and abuse of people based upon their body shape, their hair color, physical challenges, how they identified as human beings, how much money they made or didn't make, what kind of automobile they drove, the neighborhood where they lived, and on and on. My older son is left-handed. Had he been born only a few years before he was, in many schools, he would have been forced to learn to write with his right hand (as if left-handed people were somehow inferior).

"Dogs get it!" the man on 49th Street said. Mine was a brief encounter with him and the Poodle owner, but an important one for me. At least a couple of takeaways were clear and obvious truths that can make life better and different if I pay attention.

For starters, the seemingly dissimilar dogs delighting in each other reminded me that *[1] People are like seasoning in the soup of life. Differences make it tasty*. Burns and Allen. Martin and Lewis. Nichols and May. Rowan and Martin. Who wants to watch a comedy duo with two straight men or with two comics competing for laughs? It is the interplay between two distinctively different characters that creates the humor. Rogers and Hammerstein. Rogers and Hart. Carole King and Gerry Coffin. Bernie Taupin and Elton

John. Burt Bacharach and Hal David. The collaboration of the lyricist with the composer creates music. I love to play in the kitchen and have concocted, among other things, a pretty mean recipe for pie filling that works just as well with pears as it does with apples. But apples or pears alone do not make a pie. It also requires butter, nutmeg, cinnamon, brown sugar, and pastry (along with a couple of other ingredients that friends keep inquiring about but I continue to guard as a secret).

So it is with relationships. How much we would lose if we were all human versions of Spaniels with no Poodles to be found. Who would long remain satisfied living among a community of Stepford clones where everyone looks alike, dresses alike, acts alike, thinks alike, votes alike, and *is* alike in virtually all ways? The varying hues and colors of people bring artistry to life's canvas. We are not one stroke of the brush. We are a collage of countless strokes, none exactly like the other, that turn the canvas into something magic and alive. Bass and soprano. Pitcher and catcher. Teacher and student. Old and young. Black and brown and white. Female and male. The list is without end, and those who are wise respond with delight, *"Viva la difference!"* Each of us is one piece of a large puzzle. We need one another to be made whole ... and to be made happy.

Another lesson that emerged from the canine encounter was that *[2] I cheat myself when I keep relationships confined within tight parameters*. If I rigidly relate only to those of "the same breed," my life is diminished. If I enter into discourse simply with others who share my points of view, then my philosophy of life never has a chance to grow or mature. In a gym, weight training challenges our muscles and, thus, they grow. The same principle holds true with our mental or emotional muscles. Challenging ourselves by considering opinions other than our own, whether or not those opinions convert us, serves to broaden and deepen our worldview. And that is virtually always life-enhancing.

Two friends of many years are on opposite ends of the political spectrum. Neither is hostile or irrational about his personal philosophy of politics, but each is deeply committed. I agree with neither of them on all things, but do listen to each of them carefully. From one, I have heard much about economics and how neither individuals nor nations can continue to spend more than they earn *ad infinitum* and exist. From the other, I have heard about the moral imperative to care for those who cannot care for themselves (the hungry, the homeless, the infirm, the very old or very young). They differ about topics like military interventions, public education, health care, and a seemingly endless list of additional concerns. On some issues I gain wisdom from one friend, on different issues from the other. Whereas, like most people, I ordinarily reside somewhere in the middle (a brother-in-law laughingly calls me "a flaming moderate"), I have entertained and grown from ideas from each friend. And, I have been inspired to see the two of them refuse to allow politics to usurp friendship or moral imperatives. I see them side-by-side at everything from backyard barbecues to Habitat for Humanity projects to annual fishing trips to the Outer Banks.

As my two friends remind me when the topic is politics, so do others provide a similar reminder regarding numerous other topics. I know pastors, rabbis, and Imams who are as close as siblings to one another. Two of my lifelong friends (we refer to each other as "brothers") are graduates and diehard athletic fans of UNC. I have a degree from Duke. Thus, my athletic loyalties are with Carolina's chief rival. At some level we realize basketball and football are simply games, but friendship is a treasure. While in New York, a close associate used to say to me, "What sort of a person would eat grits?" I always responded, "What sort of a person would eat scrapple?" One of our joys, however, was dining together … especially at a cafe in the neighborhood that served a wonderful breakfast.

Categories that separate people are artificial constructions we build with the bricks and mortar of fear. What we do not understand, we fear. What we fear, we seek to isolate from ourselves (or insulate ourselves from them). The end result is that we discard an option at our disposal that could provide deep and lasting relationships, ultimately which would result in life rather than mere existence. "Dogs get it!" Poodles and Spaniels dare to bridge gaps of breed and, therefore, discover tail-wagging joy.

Our little dogs are gone now. They lived long and blissful lives, never closing themselves off to the possibilities of love and happiness that might come from unexpected sources. Though they are gone from us, their wisdom and lessons live on with us. We are the better for it.

The Sorrento Innkeeper

"Neither do I say you are guilty. Go your way, and do not sin again."

(John 8:11,

New Life Version)

It was June. My wife and I were in Italy on the beautiful, hilly coast of the Bay of Naples. We had traveled there for a wedding and extended our stay in order to spend some time in Sorrento, Venice, and Rome. While in Sorrento, we lodged at a small, comfortable, and charming bed-and-breakfast inn on the side of a hill. Even for a person whose business is words, I am challenged to find any adequate to describe how utterly peaceful, pleasant, and captivating that place was.

The innkeeper was a young woman, thirtyish, who managed the lodging along with her sister, one housekeeper, and her fiancé (a wonderful chef). She took a personal interest in her guests, going to unexpected lengths to ensure our comfort and to make the experience more than anyone could dare to dream of.

One day we were to board a boat for another village a few miles away. The innkeeper drove us down the small and winding roads from the B&B to the dock in town. As we traveled, she mentioned some disturbing news that emanated from the States. A political decision had been made in D.C. It had global implications, making many of our long-term allies nervous. To most folks, the rationale for the decision was difficult to understand.

"What do you think of that?" she asked as she carried us into town.

I answered, "I obviously don't know all the details. But, from what I have read, I hope the matter is resolved quickly. I feel embarrassed by what happened."

She replied with her ever-present smile and cheerful voice, "You have no need to feel that way. We don't blame you for someone else's decisions." Immediately she pointed out a lovely and expansive lemon orchard, and thankfully the topic changed.

"We don't blame you for someone else's decisions." Hers was a word of grace. It was also a word of wisdom that I often need to remember.

Two takeaways come to mind as I reflect on that moment with our gentle and hospitable innkeeper. *[1] I too often blame others for things over which they do not have absolute control.* In so doing, I preclude the possibility of positive relationships.

My father was a broadcast journalist. He was a man committed to sharing truth with people, but also to sharing it in a way that was fair to all sides involved. Before airing a story that could prove detrimental to another individual, he would phone that person to advise them that the news was breaking. He would then share what was planned to be broadcast and ask for their perspective or for any additional information that might cast a new or different light on the situation. As I noted, he was committed to truth. But, also to fairness. Most people responded to his calls positively, thanking him for being considerate enough to seek their point of view before going public. Occasionally, however, there would be a different reaction. Someone caught with his hand in the till, some public servant who had taken advantage of his office and his constituents, would explode in anger when advised that his secret may not remain a secret much longer. With every expletive imaginable, he would shout at my father, "How can you do this?" Dad would always answer, as calmly and courteously as possible, "I'm not the one who did it. I'm merely the one who is reporting it."

A convicted felon may blame his environment for the crime that put him behind bars. "I never stood a chance, growing up in that neighborhood," he argues. And that argument that should not be summarily dismissed. There are those who would not intentionally have chosen lives of crime but who simply went along with a crowd that was moving in the wrong direction. There are those who mistakenly sensed no hope of bettering their circumstances unless they took illegal shortcuts. There are even those who did what they knew to be wrong out of fear that if they refused, they would suffer retribution. "I never had a chance!" he says. "My neighborhood determined my outcome." But if that is true, then logic would decree that every young person who grew up in that same neighborhood would wind up in a prison cell. Such simply is not the case. There are those who rise above their environment and its negative influences. There are those who become inspired not only to overcome the environment but also to change it or to lead others out of it to more positive and productive places. "Had it not been for the people who lived there, my story would be different." That statement is defensible only when others have the power to make your ultimate choices, which is almost never actually the case. It is easy to blame others for things over which, in the end, they do not have absolute control.

"How could you let this happen!" is a familiar refrain. Each of us can name numerous occasions when we have heard those words projected at people who had little or nothing to do with what happened. An acquaintance who is a weather forecaster told me that he is occasionally accosted in public places by strangers who are upset about the immensity of a storm that blew through, and they say to him: "How could you let this happen!" as if he had any control over the activities of Mother Nature.

To be sure, there are sometimes external influences that make our lives at home or at work challenging and unfulfilling. But, in every instance it is too easy to put all the blame on someone else's shoulders. A national economic downturn, for example, dampens our emotional state of mind. Our resulting dark and troubled spirit finds an outlet at home, venting our financial fears and frustrations via unkindness toward a spouse or children who have no power whatsoever over the nation's economy. An unpleasant client makes us angry and defensive, whereupon we take out those feelings on our employees or assistants who in no way stimulated or supported the abrasive behavior that caused our bad mood. The list of examples goes on and on. The point is simply that too often we blame others for things over which they have little or no control. That is never fair. And it always jeopardizes relationships.

When I apologized to the hostess in Sorrento, she replied, "You have no need to feel that way. We don't blame you for someone else's decisions." Another valid and valuable lesson her words taught me was this: *[2] I too often blame myself for things over which I do not have absolute control ... or about things in the past that I cannot call back and do-over.*

"How could you let that happen!" is a phrase that often unfairly projects blame onto others. "Sorry about that" is a phrase that often accepts blame for circumstances beyond our control. The words flow so easily when we are with someone else who steps off the curb into a puddle or bites into a burger and gets a mustard stain on her blouse or bumps his head getting into the back seat of a car. "Sorry about that," we say, as if we did something to cause their misfortune. But, we didn't. When we have no responsibility for something, we have no reason to apologize for it.

Obviously the phrase "Sorry about that" does not usually imply a sense of personal remorse or responsibility. It's just a way of standing with someone in a moment of their hardship, acknowledging it, and expressing concern or compassion. Nonetheless, the phrase itself does imply a truth about so many of us: that we too often live under unwarranted umbrellas of guilt. Somewhere at some time, someone taught us to think more poorly of ourselves than we ever ought to think.

Rarely do I refer to the topic of *forgiveness* without having someone in the congregation or audience confess to me in private that their greatest obstacle is learning to forgive not others but themselves. Often, the person will tell me their story as if it is the darkest and most sinister story I have ever heard. It almost never is. A poet phrased it well:

> *Once in a saintly passion*
> *I cried with desperate grief,*
> *"O Lord, my heart is black with guile,*
> *Of sinners I am chief."*

Then stooped my guardian angel
And whispered from behind,
"Vanity, my little man,
You're nothing of the kind."
(*Once In a Saintly Passion*, James Thomson)

There are very few things any of us have ever done that makes us dark and sinister. At worst, most of us are merely broken and human. Have we made mistakes, errors in judgment, and have some of those mistakes had irretrievably negative consequences? Yes. But in processing those memories, we really only have two options: either to be immobilized or to be equipped. We either surrender to the chains of guilt that hold us forever captive, or we learn from bad decisions in order to move forward and make better ones in times to come. As I teach my students in Practical Theology, guilt can be one of only two things: a prison cell or a classroom. It either confines and restricts us, preventing our discovering meaning and joy. Or, it equips and empowers us, teaching valuable lessons about what roads not to walk in the future that took us to unfortunate places in the past.

An acquaintance spent time in prison for selling drugs. He now works as a community activist and substance abuse counselor. He allowed a bad memory to inspire him toward a noble purpose. Another also spent time behind bars for embezzlement. Upon his release, he went to grad school, attained a Masters Degree in Theology, and now serves as a chaplain in the very prison unit where he once was an inmate. We could all articulate similar stories, sometimes a bit less dramatic but no less important. We all know people who, to use the cliché, actually did turn lemons into lemonades. They learned the lessons that bad decisions can teach, lessons that help us make good decisions later on.

A professional golfer I knew told of watching hours of videotapes of his performance on the links. He was a good golfer who had never managed to break through with a victory, but rather always seemed to finish in the middle of the pack. His short irons from a level lie or uphill lie were his nemesis. He was great off the tee and could putt as well as anyone on the tour. He was good with long irons and out of bunkers. He could even hit his 9-iron and wedge shots accurately from a downhill lie, getting proper loft and creating that artistic spin that sends the ball past the hole and then turns it back to within inches of its target. But if he stood level to or on a slope higher than the green, he could use those same irons and the results would be erratic (and often disastrous). He couldn't get the proper loft or spin. He would hit one shot embarrassingly short of the flag and the next so far past it that it would roll off the other side of the green. That one area of his game prevented him from being a contender and kept him in the ranks of also-rans.

While watching the videotapes, the golfer noticed something about his stance. On every shot, his feet were set in a certain way that allowed his weight to shift naturally from backswing to impact to follow-through. However, when he was near the green but standing level with or higher than its surface, without being aware he would shift his front foot to put more weight on it. Over and over he saw himself doing that, most always with undesired results. The slight shift of stance altered the quality of his swing, accounting for the inaccuracy of those shots. Over the course of a round of eighteen holes, that alone often added three or four strokes to his score. Over the course of a four-day tournament, those accumulated strokes always took him out of contention.

The golfer, having seen the mistake he had consistently made, began to practice that one stroke. He applied himself diligently to footwork, slightly changing his stance so that his swing became smooth and natural. Within a short period of time, he moved from the middle of the pack to being a consistent challenger for tournament titles, even winning his first championship at a course where he had never played well before. In recalling that learning experience, he wrote that initially he felt regret bordering on heartbreak for all the missed chances he had squandered in the past. If only he had watched videos earlier! If only he had figured out the difference his stance could make! He could have won any number of trophies. He could have been a superstar. Soon enough, though, reason took over and he realized that yesterday cannot be recalled or repaired. However, having learned its tough lessons, he also realized that he could make sufficient changes in what he was doing to achieve different results in his tomorrows. His past mistakes became teachable moments. Learning from them, he became a champion.

We often blame ourselves for things over which we have no control. But perhaps more often, we punish ourselves for things over which we once had control but no longer do.

The Moving Finger writes; and, having writ,

Moves on: nor all thy Piety nor Wit

Shall lure it back to cancel half a Line,

Nor all thy Tears wash out a Word of it.

(Edward Fitzgerald, *The Rubaiyat of Omar Khayyam*, Boston: Houghton, Mifflin and Company, 1887)

We cannot undo what has been done. We cannot unsay what has been said. We cannot cancel even half a line of what we did or failed to do in times past. But, we can examine and assess. We can listen to the voice of guilt or failure until it has taught us what it has to teach, and then we can (and should) bid it goodbye and move forward. Only then can we put its lessons to use in building the kind of future we won't have to feel guilty about or disappointed in. To blame ourselves for things over which we had no control is foolish and a waste of energy. It is no less foolish, however, to allow ourselves to remain forever held captive by mistakes for which we were, in fact, responsible in the past, things that can neither be retrieved nor repaired. Learn the lessons. Then let the rest go. Life at its best is a movement forward. Choosing to carry the burden of remorse is like trying to drive forward with your gear shift in reverse.

One of the finest and most dedicated physicians I know almost left the profession years ago when he lost a certain patient. She was a dear woman, a close friend of his and of mine.

Every doctor loses patients. They understand the dynamics of terminal illnesses when they choose to enter the profession. If every doctor abandoned their practice when they lost a patient, no physician would practice very long. However, in the case of that particular physician who almost hung up his stethoscope, he misdiagnosed the case. It was tricky. The illness was rare and hid itself in a way that common X-rays would not reveal. The doctor treated her symptoms as most physicians would have. As the symptoms grew worse, he changed to other medications designed to treat the same disorder he had originally diagnosed. Only upon admission to a hospital where additional, complex diagnostic procedures took place was it revealed that something entirely different was going on. By that time, it was too late to reverse it. We watched a dear and gentle wife and mom die. Perhaps she would have anyway, as the illness from which she suffered is frequently a deadly one. But the physician blamed himself, convinced that had he been more diligent in ordering tests and had he discovered the real ailment early on, he could have saved her. So, the sensitive man that he is, he fell into a depression and seriously contemplated walking away from his life in medicine.

Countless voices (friends who know him, patients who need him, physicians who respect him, and family who love him) prevailed upon the man to remain in his profession. So, he did. Other doctors associated with him attest that he has become the best and most thorough diagnostician in their city. He virtually never misses anything, going to unusual lengths to make certain what he is actually treating before the treatments begin. A tragic experience, one that could not be recalled or reversed, taught him a valuable lesson that has no doubt saved countless lives across the years and continues to do so.

Sometimes, we learn tough lessons that help us build good lives. "We don't blame you for someone else's decisions," said the sweet Sorrento innkeeper. Our predilection to cast blame (at others or at self) almost never leads in the direction of wholeness, happiness, or hope. Rather, it is the determination to move forward free of resentment toward another and free of guilt regarding our own past that propels us in the direction of life in its fullness.

The Restaurateur

"A soft answer turns away wrath, but a harsh word stirs up anger."

(Proverbs 15:1,
Revised Standard Version)

The owner of the restaurant approached my table. "Nice to see you again," he said, extending his hand. "It's been a long time."

I smiled and told him I was happy to be there. He continued, mentioning a professional colleague of mine. "He comes every week, sometimes twice. He brings staff members and friends. You're rarely here at all. I am working hard to succeed in this city. Why do you not wish to help me?"

How do you respond in moments like those? Having grown up in a nice southern town with churches on every corner, surrounded by all the values implicit in that, I have always possessed well-nourished senses of duty and guilt. Surely everything is either (a) up to me or (b) somehow my fault. I feel an inner kinship with those burdened believers who belong to the fictional church from *A Prairie Home Companion*, "Our Lady of Perpetual Responsibility." So, here was a restaurant and bar owner who claimed to be struggling in New York City, clearly unhappy that I did not bring friends to dine there more often. The tapes inside my head began playing, assuring the child within that the restaurateur's success was my responsibility or, conversely, that his failure was my fault.

The logical voices in my head reminded me that there were other, far more honest responses available that could be made. For example, I could have countered that one individual person (even one who occasionally brings friends) does not have a make-or-break impact on dining establishments. There is a difference between a client and a clientele.

Or, I could have pointed out that whatever broiled fish he served always tasted blandly like every other broiled fish he served. There was really no need to list "sea bass," "grouper," "red snapper," or anything else on the menu. Just be honest and let it say "fish." It was all the same.

Just a piece of white, flavorless fish with a couple of stalks of broccoli on the side.

Or, I could have mentioned that his "homemade marinara" was obviously Prego or Ragu. I have nothing against either brand and use them frequently. But when I dine at an expensive restaurant that claims to be "authentic northern Italian," I assume "homemade" marinara does not come from a jar available on the shelf of the grocery next door.

Or, I could have made the logical point that perhaps my colleague whom he mentioned and I have differing tastes in food. We do not dress like nine-year-old identical twins. We do not drive the same automobiles. He likes Opera, I like James Taylor, Gillian Welch, and the Tams. So, is it conceivable that our taste buds are not engineered in precisely the same way? Maybe he has a thing for bland broiled fish. Maybe I have a thing for dishes that are a bit spicier.

Or, I could have responded that when one orders a piece of broiled fish with two stalks of broccoli, a small dish of olives, one piece of bread, and a glass of unsweetened tea, maybe a check for eighty dollars seems a bit excessive. In fact, had he seriously considered it, he could have been led to wonder if I chose to eat more frequently at other places because their food was better and their prices were more affordable.

Or, I could simply have pointed out that when a diner enters a restaurant and is treated rudely and chastised for not spending his money there often enough to please the owner, it does not ignite a flame of yearning to be a regular patron. Perhaps that could have been a teachable moment, helping him understand that honey really does attract more flies than vinegar and that simple courtesy is a fundamental building block in constructing a healthy business.

What do we do when people project expectations or responsibilities on us that are unreasonable? In terms of human relationships, whereas I believe in being honest and forthright, I always assess which battles are worth the fight. Sometimes when two people have an unpleasant confrontation, fighting fire with fire only results in a bigger blaze. There's an adage: "You don't have to attend every fight to which you are invited." Good advice. I had not come to his place for an argument. I had simply stopped in for lunch. So I reiterated my statement from the beginning, telling him how happy I was to be there and how much I was looking forward to the meal. Then, before he could extend his tirade, I asked him if there were any Specials that day that didn't show up on the menu. He called for a table server and walked away. Eventually I wound up saying, "Just bring me the fish." It really didn't seem to matter what kind it was.

Many of the best lessons, things that benefit us to know and practice, are taught to us as children. We learn them at home, at school, in synagogue or church, from Grandma or the coach or the nanny. But, there are also other lessons that should not be carried into adult life. We are taught to be "nice," as well we should be. But, being nice to people does not mean I am responsible for their lives or behaviors. We are taught to be sensitive, and that is a vital lesson. But, being sensitive to others does not mean I am necessarily at fault when they fall on their faces. We are taught to be loving, and there is no higher virtue. But, loving my neighbor as myself does not mean loving my neighbor at the expense of myself (becoming a victim or a doormat).

A friend of many years (who could easily be captain of any codependency team on the planet) said to me, "I often feel like I carry the weight of the world on my shoulders, but most of that weight does not belong to me." It was a healthy insight into his long journey to emotional liberation. We love, we care, we share, we help, we give, we listen, we encourage, but we are not ultimately responsible for how anyone else turns out, for their successes or their failures, their joys or their heartaches. I make my world a better place to the best of my ability, but I cannot necessarily recreate your world. Hopefully I shine a positive light on it, but at the end of the day, your world is yours to manage.

The owner of the restaurant was responsible for his food, his menu, his pricing, his advertising, his staff, his ambiance, and his way of greeting and welcoming customers. The frequency of my eating there had little to do with whether or not he succeeded in fulfilling those responsibilities. My emotional temptation to assume responsibility was illogical. I am neither his problem nor his deliverer. I am just one man who stopped in for lunch. How often I choose to dine there is my business. How he treats me as a customer is his. Whether he succeeds or fails as a restaurateur is his business, as well, not my responsibility. That was confirmed to me by the fact that since that day I never returned to his establishment, and yet the restaurant is still in business. Apparently my support or lack thereof was never the issue, and it was foolish (even for a brief moment) for me to feel otherwise.

Takeaway: *We bear no guilt for negativity in our neighbors. We are simply responsible for treating people positively.* We are responsible for how we deal with others, how we speak to them and of them, for never using or abusing, for being honest and fair, for refraining from violence or vitriol. Those are our behavioral responsibilities and should be taken seriously and honored. We are never endowed with a license to be cruel or unkind. But, we are not accountable for the worldview of other individuals, for their initiative or lethargy, for their success or failure, for their determination or apathy. If someone is unkind to me, that is their problem. I am liable only for how I choose to respond.

There are times when I simply do not agree with another person's position. I can argue, if I choose. Or, I can use relational language that retains the option for ongoing, constructive dialog: "I hear what you're saying," or "That's certainly one way of looking at it," or "I can see you are a person of deep conviction," or even, "I guess we'll just have to agree to disagree."

There are times when another person's actions cross a discernible and indefensible line. In those moments it is both understandable and probably wise to say, "Your words are hurtful." "What you just did is painful." "I suspect you didn't intend to wound me, but that's how I feel."

There are times when it makes sense simply to walk away. There is no shame in that, no cowardice implied. When another person has reached a point of anger that transcends our ability to reason with it, it is often best simply to say, "I value our relationship too much to jeopardize it. So, once things have cooled off and we can be reasonable, let's talk." Then, turn and walk away. If they keep talking, you keep walking.

And, there are times when it just isn't that important. Therefore, rather than respond to his complaints, I simply said to the owner of the restaurant, "Are there any Specials today that don't show up on the menu?" As it turned out, the Special was fish.

Friends We Haven't Met Yet

"Offer hospitality to one another without grumbling."

(I Peter 4:9,

New International Version)

I had been invited to speak at a fundraising event for a large retirement community in New Jersey. The organizers were incredibly accommodating, the venue was magnificent, the musical guests were world-class, the food was gourmet, and the evening promised to be the sort of glitz-and-glamor occasion that one does not typically associate either with retirement communities or, I suspect, with me. But there we were, my wife and I, enjoying every minute and every aspect of the night.

During the cocktail hour preceding dinner, we schmoozed (as expected) with the prospective donors throughout the room. After making certain that no one had been ignored, we found a table where we could sit, nibble our shrimp and cheese, and where I could gather my thoughts regarding the address I was about to deliver.

We had only been at the table for a minute or so when a couple approached and asked if they could sit with us. They were advanced in years. She was seated in a wheelchair that he carefully and lovingly placed at the table before taking his seat. They introduced themselves not as prospective donors but rather as residents of the retirement community. Numerous residential couples and individuals had been invited to the dinner so that prospective donors could meet and interact with those whom they were being asked to assist. We exchanged brief pleasantries. Then the wife smiled warmly and said, "You don't know us, but we are your friends. We watch you every week on TV."

"You don't know us, but we are your friends." We had never met. I did not know their names or their stories. And yet, to them I was a "friend." Someone they knew. Someone they took seriously. Someone they trusted. In fact, someone they welcomed into their home on a weekly basis.

Every day in the Piedmont area of the state where I grew up, people listened to my father on the radio. They believed what he told them. They believed in him. Often at restaurants, strangers would approach our table and introduce themselves. I can hear them as clearly in my memory now as I heard them while seated at those tables years ago. "We heard your voice and knew it was you. We just had to come over and say 'Hello.' We listen to you every day."

To me, they were interruptions. This was our family time. Our time for conversation and connection. This was my time to share joys and concerns about school, friendships, scouts, and little league with my parents. But, folks we didn't even know were disrupting that.

"Dad," I would sometimes ask, "why do we have to stop eating and talking and let these people be such a nuisance? We don't know them. Why do you treat them like we do?"

Again, I can hear his answer as clearly now as I did then. "They are strangers to us, son. But I'm not a stranger to them. I am a guest in their home every day. They should be just as welcome at my table as they make me in their home."

"You don't know us, but we are your friends." We all have friends we haven't met yet, people we do not know but who know something about us. My parents understood that. In time, I have come to understand it as well.

Three takeaways come to mind from brief moments my wife and I shared during a cocktail hour with two gracious people who thought of me as a friend.

[1] Someone is watching. "We watch you every week on TV." They observed my life. They heard my stories. They listened to my opinions and philosophies. And apparently, the felt all that somehow contributed to their understanding of Truth.

TV or no TV, we are all observed. It happens in places of business, neighborhoods, civic arenas, at homes (or in extended families), casual relationships, public places (like stores or theaters). Whenever we are not alone, people pay attention to who we are, what we say, how we say it, what we do, and how we treat others around us. When that happens, the examples they witness from us can serve as sources of inspiration, disappointment, and/or modeling (an example that influences their behavior).

Standing in a long checkout line at a grocery store, I observed the interaction between the shopper ahead of me and the cashier. The shopper was handed some change after paying.

She looked at it, turned to the cashier and said, "You gave me too much money back. You owed me thirty-five cents. You gave me a dollar and thirty-five cents. You need to take this dollar." The cashier, obviously feeling rushed and pressured by the long line of people in a hurry, had miscalculated when she gave it to her. Just as obviously, she was surprised by the customer's honesty.

"Thank you for doing that," she said. "Some people would have just pocketed that extra dollar and said nothing. And I wouldn't have known until we balanced things at the end of the day. It would have come out of my wages."

The customer smiled. "I have to live with myself," she answered. "That's not easy to do when you take advantage of people—even if it's only a dollar."

When she was gone and I stepped up in line, the cashier said to me, "I wish everyone were like that woman. I need to be more like her myself." Then she began ringing up my purchases, after which I made certain she had not returned to me too much change. In short, both the cashier and I were inspired by the woman who did the right thing simply because it was the right thing to do. Each of us realized in the woman's act that our moral character is revealed in how we treat others, how we refuse to take advantage of their mistakes, and how we stand fast on ethical principles at all times in all places. "I need to be more like her myself," said the cashier, and I said a silent "Amen" about my own life.

Others are watching us, even when we do not know. At our best, they see sources of inspiration in us, to become their best. Hopefully their actions are then observed by others who likewise replicate what they see until the old ripple effect takes place.

The opposite is, unfortunately, also true. Our misdeeds are observed and become sources of disappointment or discouragement to others. Had the shopper in front of me kept the dollar, and had I somehow been aware, I may have thought, "It's right what people often say—no one can be trusted. We're all in it just for ourselves." The likelihood of my having known that she received and kept inaccurate change is incredibly small. But, it is highly likely bordering on certain that I will witness negative human actions and interactions on a daily basis. I can observe the way supervisors at work speak to their employees. I can observe road rage. I can observe expressions of hostility or hear statements of racism. I can read tweets that are demeaning or divisive. I can see people treat others with disrespect or impatience. I can witness orchestrated efforts to beat the system at the expense of strangers. I can stand on a street corner and be exposed to another's obscene rants of anger into a cell phone. I can be aware of sexism, misogyny, or abuse. Come up with your own list. It will be a long one, all examples of people sinking to low levels of behavior rather than rising to high ones. Every time, someone is watching. And that someone is being influenced to think, as Bruce Hornsby sang, "That's just the way it is." (*The Way It Is*, RCA Records, 1986) Everybody does it. Why shouldn't I? And little by little the cumulative effect is that we give up on the dreams of morality, civility, kindness, and human compassion. We stop believing in the possibility of becoming our best selves and, thus, settle for a sort of existence that isn't authentic living at all.

Others are watching us. When they see us failing to live up to best standards, they quit believing that the best is actually a possibility.

To be sure, wherever our behavior lands on the spectrum from exemplary to atrocious, it will become the model for someone else to follow. Every parent should know this. Whether mafia boss or gentle-natured caregiver, chances are high that your children will grow in the direction of what and who you are. That is almost inevitable. We plant the seeds. Then the flower grows.

Do you advise your young children to stay clear of the use of drugs? And, do those children see you frequently inebriated? Do you tell your children to respect other people? And, do your children hear you make denigrating remarks or jokes about others based on their color, sexuality, economics, body shapes, or politics? Do you want your children to remain physically healthy? And, do your children watch you smoke? "Do as I say, not as I do" never produces the desired results. People in the process of shaping their life-values do as we do. We are their models. Their examples. Being such carries with it enormous responsibility.

Whether we know it or not, we are all being observed. And what others see in us become sources of inspiration, disappointment, or examples to follow.

[2] We matter to someone. "You don't know us, but we are your friends," she said. That is a cherished gift, one not to be taken lightly.

A friend, it is frequently said, is someone who comes in when all others are going out. In other words, a friend is someone who stands with you. They've got your back. They believe in you, cheer for you, weep when you weep and dance when you dance. A friend will be honest, but always in a kind way. A friend will be sympathetic, but never in a paternal way. A friend simply loves you as you are and asks only that you return the favor.

That couple, those friends I hadn't met yet, confessed that I mattered to them. As a weekly on-screen guest in their home, I had some in their lives. They listened to me. They took my thoughts seriously. They respected what I said, which meant they respected who I am. Those are not favors to be lightly considered.

In its political Cabinet, Great Britain has created a position called Minister of Loneliness. Kudos to them. In our own nation, it is estimated that as many as 75% of American adults feel some measure of loneliness. Maybe a similar Cabinet-level position would not be such a bad idea. Loneliness is fundamentally to feel disconnected. That ranges from feeling misunderstood to feeling marginalized to feeling virtually invisible. But wherever one may fall on that linear measuring rod, becoming aware that you matter to someone (if only to just one person) is an effective antidote for loneliness.

Frequently we simply do not know the extent to which we actually matter to someone else. Prior to our time that night at an *hor d'oeuvre* table, I had no idea those two retired adults in New Jersey existed (let alone that I was a meaningful presence in their lives). Whether or not we are aware, however, we are important and impactful in someone else's eyes and estimation. There is someone who cares about you and would offer renewing and empowering friendship given the chance. Sometimes you just haven't met them yet.

[3] Kindness is not a lot to ask. "May we sit with you?," they inquired tentatively. In all honesty, I had spoken all the Hellos I desired to say by that point. I really wanted to focus on other words I would soon be speaking to a gathered audience. But here was an aged couple, one in a wheelchair, asking only if for a few minutes they could share a table with strangers. It wasn't as if they requested that I paint their house or rebuild their automobile engine. They simply said, "May we sit with you?"

Most people neither ask nor expect anything that demands too much from us. They simply hope to be treated with compassion and gentleness. They long to be listened to. Looked at. Smiled at. Acknowledged. Respected.

"We heard your voice and knew it was you," strangers would say as they approached the table where Mom, Dad, and I sat years ago. "We just had to come over and say 'Hello.' We listen to you every day." It would have been rude-bordering-on-cruel had my father responded, "Go away. Can't you see I'm having dinner with my family? I don't have time to be interrupted." But he and Mom understood that we always have time to express kindness. If we are ever too busy to be kind, then we are indeed too busy. It cost them nothing to be polite and patient with another human being. And, in fact, doing so gave both of my parents a sense of gladness. One of the inevitable results of extending kindness to others is that we discover joy in the process. Happiness is one of the few commodities we find only by giving it away.

Kindness is never a lot to ask of us. It only requires treating the other person the way we would want to be treated were the tables turned. In the Latin, the word "compassion" means "to suffer with." To feel pain when others are in pain. For our purposes, it can mean simply to put ourselves in the other's place. To imagine how it feels to be that person. One thing we can be certain of, no matter what individual (friend or stranger) we're talking about, is this: She or he is wounded in some way. It may not show. They may have gone to great lengths to disguise it. But everyone is bearing up under something. Kindness helps them to keep moving forward. Rejection, judgment, or apathy deepens the wound. It costs us almost nothing to be a momentary ray of light that dispels someone else's shadows or, at least, makes their shadows a bit easier to survive.

"You don't know us, but we are your friends." We never saw them again after that night, but we did receive their letters from time to time. The letters were always encouraging and affirming. They became people we, also, thought of as friends. That night at a table during the cocktail hour, we had no way of knowing what the future would hold. They came to us as friends we hadn't met yet. We all have such persons in our orbs of existence. Be aware of that. Celebrate it. Some of your deepest and most lasting relationships may be just around the bend.

I Hear The Beauty

"My dear brothers and sisters, take note of this: Everyone should be quick to listen (and) slow to speak ...."

(James 1:19,

New International Version)

December in New York City is a magic time. December in any city is a magic time, but I've spent a lot of Decembers in NYC. The concerts. The lighting of the tree at Rockefeller Plaza. The Christmas extravaganza at Radio City Music Hall. The way the Village is dressed. The tourists. The store windows.

I especially love the store windows. It's one of the city's free gifts to all of us, as store by store, they seek to outshine one another. Saks. Bergdorf-Goodman. Bloomingdale's (which, just prior to revealing its newly decorated windows, offers the public a free concert with people like Harry Connick, Jr. or John Legend). Always one of my favorites (which, sadly, is no longer there) was Lord and Taylor on 5th at 39th.

Much like a tourist, I lingered in front of Lord and Taylor on a cold evening in early December. Slowly I was taking in each detail of each decorated window, one window at a time. As I stood in front of a certain one that appeared to be a colorfully, mechanized scene right out of a Dickens novel, the man standing beside me said, "It's beautiful, isn't it?"

When I turned to respond, I noticed that he was wearing dark glasses at night and carried a red-tipped cane. Obviously visually impaired to the point of being legally blind, I assumed he could still see at least a bit of the decorations before him. Why else would he be standing there? Why else his remark about the window's beauty?

"It really is beautiful," I replied. Then I continued, "Forgive me for being too personal, but how much of the window are you able to see?"

"None," he answered. "I *hear* the beauty."

"I hear the beauty." To be said by a patron of the symphony is one thing, but to be said by a sightless man in front of a Christmas window is quite another. Since he seemed willing to chat, I decided to inquire.

"What an intriguing phrase. I'm not sure I have heard someone use it before, at least, not about windows. Can you explain that a little for me? How can you hear what was created to be seen?"

"Lots of ways," he answered with a smile. "For starters, close your eyes and listen for a second." I did as he asked. "Now," he said, "tell me what you hear."

"I hear music. *Good King Wenceslas*, to be exact."

"Very good," the gentleman complimented. "Christmas music is my favorite kind of all. Sometimes I play Christmas CDs in March or August, just because I love the music so much. This month I'm surrounded by it. I often ask people to describe a window to me. When they do, I get a mental picture and can imagine the movement of each character, its speed and fluidity, by listening to the pace of the music. It helps me create beautiful scenes in my head. Who knows? Some of them may be prettier than the actual ones in the window. Now, close your eyes again and listen." Once more, I did as he asked.

"Tell me anything you hear," he advised.

"I hear a siren going by," I answered.

"True," the man continued. "But, that's a distraction. What I want you to do is to tell me anything you hear that is directly related to this window."

It only took a second until a child's voice, a little girl, spoke. "Mommy, look at how that princess twirls. She's dancing in the snow. And that prince is going to dance with her sometime, too, isn't he?"

"A child," I told him. "I hear a child describing the scene to her mother."

"Part of the scene," he corrected. "The whole window is more than one dancing figurine. But, you're correct. You just got an image of part of the scene. And, you received something else. What was it?"

I felt like a student in a first-year college class on Art or Literature. "What do you hear in the poem?" the professor would push. And so I sought to answer this street-corner blind man who had become my impromptu professor. "I hear excitement. She's thrilled by something she sees in this window."

"Yes!" he said with a discernible note of enthusiasm. "You hear excitement. What else?"

"I don't know. I just know she's happy about the window and is expressing that to her mother."

"You hear family," he answered. "You just said so. She is telling her mother how much the window thrills her. You have just heard a bit of the scene in the window: excitement and family. Two very special things, my friend. Now tell me, what else?"

"You're better at this than I am," I confessed.

"I've had more practice," he said with an elfish grin.

"You tell me," I replied. "I want to know what you heard that I missed."

"I heard patience. The mother's response to her child was soft and tender. It's December. My guess is that the mother is rushed and busy. She's a family person. Gifts to buy. Parties to plan. Budgets to manage. Homework to supervise. Probably a husband sitting home right now, wondering where they both are. But, she allowed her daughter to linger and see whatever was there for a little girl to see. So, you heard patience.

"And," he went on, "you heard love—from daughter to mom and from mom to daughter."

"Yes," I agreed. "I felt that. Obviously I didn't articulate it like you have, but I did feel it."

"Man," he said, "what you felt was … Christmas! Right here in front of this window. Decorations. Music. Family. Excitement. Patience. Love. All right here at one window on Fifth Avenue. And you experienced all of it without even opening your eyes. See what I mean? I hear the beauty."

"Would you like me to describe the scene in this window?" I asked. "I mean, there's a lot more here than that one princess dancing in the snow."

"No thanks. I've been here several times. By now, I could describe every one of these windows to you. I know what people say they look like, and I know what they look like to me. So now I stand and listen for the rest of it, like what you just heard. You can listen to a hundred conversations in front of any one of these windows in a single night, and everyone is a new story. Hey, listen! *Silent Night*. That's my favorite!"

I walked on to view the other windows. He remained behind to hear his holiday favorite. Perhaps he learned from other window-shoppers, overhearing their remarks and assessments as they looked at the magic behind the glass. Or perhaps, as had just been the case with me, they learned from him.

Insight and inspiration are both sensory *and* cerebral. That was my takeaway from a magical moment with a sightless man who saw more in a Christmas window than I did. *You see (discover beauty and come to a clearer understanding of reality and mystery) by looking, hearing, smelling, and touching, but often just as much by imagining.* That night I learned a small bit of how to see with my eyes closed. My father was a broadcast journalist. He began his career during the era when radio was king. Television was soon to supplant it, but Dad was a die-hard. Until his death in 2003, he consistently contended that radio dramas engaged the imagination in ways TV never could. "Television makes it too easy," he would say. "It does your thinking for you. A drama on radio challenges you to envision the setting, the characters, how the action looks. You become part of the creative team, part of the telling of the story."

I think Dad was right. He and that man in front of the Lord and Taylor windows understood what many of us have not quite yet figured out. If we tune into life, there are ways to hear the beauty.

A Girl On A Park Bench

"Be strong and courageous. Do not be afraid; do not be discouraged, for the Lord you God will be with you wherever you go."

(Joshua 1:9,

New International Version)

Springs in Central Park are lovely occasions. Winters in the city, as in many cities, can be long and dreary with hints of spring that only serve to get your hopes up before dashing them with the next snow. So when spring finally arrives, and the trees and grass turn green, and the air is fresh, and the flowers bloom, the pathways in the park are healing places.

You can count on moms with strollers and young folks tossing Frisbees and street musicians playing guitars or saxophones. Skaters rush by, painters display their wares, and The Strand sets up its used book stand on the corner beside the rock wall. People gather in the park in spring, resurrected from apartments and offices where they have endured the long, cold days of winter. Thus, you can count on lots of laughter and newly rediscovered smiles.

I suppose the upbeat ambiance one anticipates on a spring day in the park made the presence of the young woman on the bench all the more surprising. She appeared to be in her early to mid-twenties. She wore neat and faintly Bohemian attire. Her long black hair was tied in a ponytail. Was she a student who had grown up in the city and attended one of our colleges but dreamed of faraway places with more sunshine and exotic names? Was she an aspiring actress fresh into town from Missouri or Montana, told by all who watched her sing and dance in her high school productions that she was a shoo-in for success? But in this town, did she find herself surrounded by hundreds of others with just as much talent and just as little work? Was she an employee in a bookstore, a clerk at the Paris Theater on 59th, a table server, a would-be fashion designer, a new bride? I have no idea what she did, but one look told me who she was. She was a young woman alone and in pain.

She sat on a bench in that lovely park on a warm and beautiful spring day, surrounded by countless laughing people who were breathing in the smell of fresh grass. And she wept. People strolled and skated by, apparently without noticing. Probably I noticed only by accident. I could just as easily have been looking in the other direction to see if the kid would catch the football his dad had just thrown. But instead I happened to look in her direction, and I saw a young woman, about the age of my own children, sitting by herself, crying. She was stooped from the waist, her face resting on hands with fingers spread, and those hands wet with tears.

Perhaps it was the parent in me that caused me to intrude into her world. I had not been invited. I was a stranger to her, and we don't always trust strangers, especially when we feel wounded or vulnerable. But she looked so fragile and alone, and her tears were so real and compelling. So I paused in front of her bench and posed a single question, "May I help you somehow?"

At first, she didn't even raise her face so that our eyes could meet. She kept staring at her feet and answered in almost a whisper, "No one can help me."

Reaching into my pocket, I handed her a card. "This," I said, "has my name, phone number, and professional position. If I can do something for you, or if I can help you find the right person to do something, call me."

This time she did raise her head, but only for a moment. Her freckled face was red and her nose runny from crying. She looked very much like a child whose heart had been broken.

"Thank you," she answered, with no discernible hint of emotion. Tucking the card into her blouse, she once more lowered her head, gently letting me know that our session together was concluded.

"No one can help me." That's quite a mouthful. Sadly, the emotion captured in those words is by no means unique to that crying girl in the park. "No one can help me." When someone receives a devastating diagnosis, a sense of utter helplessness is among the first feelings ordinarily experienced. "No one can help me." When someone is betrayed by a trusted friend or abandoned by a cherished lover, the feeling is the same. When a job is lost and the mortgage is due, when an arrest is made and the evidence is convincing, when a loved one dies and grief floods in, despair is often one's first companion. This situation cannot be fixed. This problem cannot be remedied. This relationship cannot be repaired. This dream cannot be realized. This guilt cannot be assuaged. This deed cannot be undone, nor can the damage it caused. "No one can help me."

And yet, if that were literally true, what are "helping professions" for? Why have therapists or physicians or clergy or financial counselors or life coaches or parole officers or A.A. sponsors or close friends or new dawns or spring flowers in the park after a long journey through winter? Maybe it is true that not every relationship will be restored. But, does that dictate that any possibility for new, different, and meaningful relationships is somehow precluded? It is true that graves will not open, enabling lost loved ones to reappear. But does that mean that our memories will forever be shrouded in grief? Or, could those memories in time become sources of joy and gratitude? Even if a diagnosis is terminal, does that prohibit someone from seizing with gusto whatever life can still be lived? Whatever a person is going through, are there not always other people within reach who can help us rediscover sunlight no matter how dark may be the clouds which surround us at the moment? "No one can help me," she whispered through her tears. But still I handed her my card, and still she tucked it into her blouse and said, "Thanks." Somehow at some deep level, even drowning in despair, the girl in the park apparently was not fully convinced of her own words. Perhaps she kept the card because she hoped against hope that she was wrong, that ultimately neither she nor any of us are ever truly beyond hope.

I sometimes think of her and of our brief encounter. Like her, there are moments when I weep. Tears become "sighs too deep for words" (Romans 8:26) and can be both cleansing and healing. There are times when I need to feel deep emotions and weep those tears alone. But, there are other moments when my pain seeks the buffer provided by the presence of people. That young woman did not go into a locked room to lie upon her bed and cry. She went to Central Park on a spring day. Instinctively she went to a place where she could not escape the presence of others had she tried, and where the ambiance of budding flowers and fresh grass provided an inescapable counterpoint to her mood. In so doing, she provided two takeaways for me. *[1] However lonely or heartbroken we may feel, we do have the option to place ourselves where others are.* And when we do that, more often than not someone will step forward to be with us, and their presence will help ameliorate our pain.

[2] The right environment can be a therapeutic force. Psychologists and physicians have long proclaimed the positive properties of

light. Music, art, and nature, likewise, possess the powers to calm our inner savage beasts. The setting she chose in which to live with her pain possessed the potential to soften the pain, maybe even to heal it. Choose to place yourself in an environment of beauty with the presence of people, and you have chosen the possibility for renewal and restoration.

Tucking my card into her blouse, she simply said, "Thank you." It wasn't much of a gift in a moment so raw with emotion. But, it was all I had to offer. Her response indicated that she understood and appreciated that. I try to remember that encounter when I am the one bent low on a park bench. I try to remember that small deeds of kindness offered by others are nonetheless kind. And kindness in any form or fashion is a sacred gift, one that makes my burden of suffering easier to carry. A gesture of love or compassion may be just that—only a gesture. But it communicates that I am not alone, that someone notices, and someone cares. In those moments, the heavens open, a ray of sun breaks through, and what seems like a little deed accomplishes a lot.

She never phoned me. Probably she felt more comfortable talking with someone from a different professional discipline. That is okay. If the card in her blouse encouraged her to call anyone else, and if that person helped dry her tears and restore her focus, then my offer was not in vain.

What Is Wrong
With These People?

"You must be born anew."

(John 3:16,

World English Bible)

"Is there some reason we just can't get along? What is wrong with these people?" What interesting questions coming from him! He's one of the most proficient guys I know, and also one of the most difficult to get along with. And there he was sounding like Rodney King.

Even those who know him casually, or at merely surface level, and know of his work history, roll their eyes when his name is mentioned. He makes unreasonable demands on everyone who works with him. He is controlling, manipulative, and intimidating. He is profane and angry, occasionally almost abusive to his workers and colleagues. He is driven, and people who are excessively driven rarely understand the wisdom of pacing one's self. Their fatigue frequently presents as impatience, and they seek to impose their exhausting work ethic on others. He is committed to always being right about everything, even those things that fall outside his experience or expertise. His ears are clearly only for decorative purposes since he never listens. Somehow he thinks everyone should be as fascinated by his world, his issues, his stories, his memories, and his successes as he is. They aren't, but it doesn't keep him from animatedly preaching to one and all about the beautiful excesses of his singularly successful life. He allows his employees to develop plans, only to announce a different plan entirely, usually advising them why all their pointless work was not well thought out. He thinks people should never question his decisions, never resist his will, never jump ship, and always gleefully hang in there due to the fact that, in truth, he does pay very well.

Obviously it all boils down to ego. Most people think his is vastly oversized. However, I suspect the exact opposite is true. I believe he is desperately trying to prove his validity to the world. Most brash and blustery folks like that man are usually trying to convince themselves of their own worth. Unless I miss my guess, his ego is paper-thin and most assuredly fragile. Though I do not know his story, I am sufficiently familiar with similar ones that I could probably venture a safe guess.

Often those who overcompensate with power or control as adults were not the golden children at home or in school.

Was his brother the golden one, the one his parents bragged about to their friends, the one who brought home all the honors and received all the accolades? Did Mom and Dad often say to him, "You should try to be more like your brother. He could teach you a few things."?

If so, then in an ironic way, his parents' prejudice became motivation for him—a passion to earn more money and achieve more awards than his brother could ever dream about and, in his success, to say: "Look at us now. Who could teach who?" But, seeds planted in childhood do not often become different flowers in adulthood. So, he still resents the love he watches his parents pour out upon his not-too-accomplished brother, who is no longer anyone's golden child. "He needs our help," they say. "You don't." They perceived the son who turned into a successful CEO to be an underachiever when he was in school. But now they perceive him to be an overachiever in adulthood. Still, though, they do not offer the praise he desires. As he sees it, they continue to prefer his brother.

Could he have been a clumsy or awkward youth, the last chosen at recess when the ball teams were picked? And did that eventuate in his total disinterest in sports, even to the point of deriding those who are interested? Since he could never have made a team in high school no matter what the sport may have been, did he at last decide that teams (and the sports they represent and the fans who support them) must be useless?

Was he the kid standing in the corner drinking punch all evening at the spring dances, afraid to ask a girl to the floor because he knew in advance how painful it is to be rejected? In adulthood, his marriages and relationships become many and fleeting. Having matured physically, he becomes quite handsome. When one mixes good looks, success, and money in the cauldron, you would expect the man of one's dreams to emerge. However, the longer any woman stays with him and the more she becomes aware of that which lies beneath the surface, the dream transforms into a nightmare. She sees, and often feels, his anger, his pain, his desperation, his manic ego that is out of control in a search for itself.

We stood in a beautiful high-rise office building with a panoramic view of the Atlantic coastline from every wall-sized window. We had just one brief encounter following a spirited meeting in the conference room. I had been invited to motivate their team toward camaraderie and unity of purpose. You know what they say about how the best-laid plans sometimes work out. This had been one of those times, and the CEO was clearly frustrated. He, of all unlikely individuals, questioned: "Is there some reason we just can't get along? What is wrong with these people?" Our brief encounter provided several takeaways.

[1] We tend to project blame rather than assume responsibility. "What is wrong with these people?" Years ago, someone going through the pain of estrangement with a family member remarked to me, "I don't understand what's up with him. I never did a single thing to hurt him, not a single thing!" In her defense, her estranged relative was not an easy man to deal with. He carried his feelings on his sleeve, he over-interpreted innocent statements and gestures, and he reacted negatively to those who made him feel less than adequate. Most who knew the man would have concurred with

her statement, "I don't understand what's up with him!" However, all those who objectively observed their dysfunctional relationship realized there were two sides to the coin. She exuded condescension. She always considered him something of an intrusion in her world and, whereas never overtly hostile, was consistently passive-aggressive toward him (as she was toward numerous others). Bottom line: There was plenty of blame to be shared. And until each party owned that, neither would take on the responsibility of doing what needed to be done to heal and restore the relationship.

Casting blame and adopting an attitude of self-righteousness only deepens divides that we wish could be bridged. A very successful manager of people (which has helped make her a very successful manager of her thriving business) coaches other business owners by saying: "Whenever conflicts arise, as they inevitably will, I look myself in the mirror and ask two questions: (1) Did I have a role in causing this? and (2) What is my role in concluding it?" Some call that "stepping up to the plate." Others call it maturity. Still others call it honesty. Whatever we call it, effective relationships (in the home, the workplace, or virtually anywhere else) are possible only when we mature past the need to always project blame and reach the point of being able to accept responsibility.

[2] *Often what irritates us most about others is that they force us to see similar qualities in ourselves*. We are frequently not self-aware. That is, of course, not new news. Almost two and a half centuries ago, Robert Burns wisely observed,

Oh would some power the gift give us,

To see ourselves as others see us.

(From "To a Louse")

Years ago, I recall hearing Bryant Kirkland say that people who are chronically late are irritated by others who keep them waiting. People who are negative are likewise annoyed by complainers. People who are self-absorbed are put off by folks who talk only about their own issues. That is because, he concluded, the people who bother us most are the ones who force us to see their characteristics in ourselves. They back us into corners where we cannot escape our own reflection. (From *Living In a Zig Zag Age*, Nashville: Abingdon Press, 1972)

What if that is not a bad thing? What if, instead, those people are our emotional tutors, teaching us valuable lessons about the effect we have on others vis-à-vis the effect we would prefer to have? A friend who is a physician shared with me something he experienced while doing Christmas shopping on Black Friday. He went to a major department store in a large mall where he knew he could make all his holiday purchases on a single day (and, in so doing, could take advantage of the store's considerable Black Friday discounts). Apparently he was not the only person in town who decided on that same course of action. As he phrased it, "Half the population of Virginia must have descended on that store that day." Due to the size of the crowd (and what he felt was a lack of preparedness on part of the store), he stood in the checkout line waiting to pay for his shopping cart full of gifts for forty-five minutes. By the time he reached the register, in his words, "I'm sure my blood pressure was so high that I would send someone else with those numbers to the ER." At the cash register, all his impatience and frustration boiled over.

The clerk said kindly, "I'm sorry for your wait. There's such a crowd today."

He replied indignantly, "You ought to be sorry! No one should have to wait forty-five minutes to be taken care of. This is unthinkable. I have other things to do with my time!"

Without raising her voice to match his and without losing her smile, the clerk replied, "I know how you feel. I guess you don't recognize me, but I was in your office two weeks ago and waited over an hour to be called back to an examining room. Then it was another half hour before you came in."

Oh would some power the gift give us,

To see ourselves as others see us.

Possibly those who annoy or frustrate us become our best teachers, revealing important personal lessons about who we are, how we deal with others, and how we might grow into better versions of ourselves.

[3] **We are the products of our pasts, but they do not have to dictate our futures**. When it comes to interpreting our pasts, we can be either immobilized or educated. It is not unlikely that the difficult CEO remained entrapped by painful memories from his childhood. And, he had not (could not? would not?) interpreted his yesterdays in such fashion as to help him construct stronger tomorrows. Because of that, his behavior based on times long gone brought pain to almost all others who crossed his path.

He is not an unintelligent man. At some level, I suspect he did not like being the sort of person he was. But, we assume, a zebra cannot change its stripes. That may be true with zebras, but it's untrue with us. Increasing work in the field of neuroscience proclaims to those who will listen: If you don't like who you are, become someone else. "How can I do that?" we reply. "It's impossible."

Neuroscience answers, "Not only is it possible, it's not even particularly difficult. You can think your way to a brand new you!"

Most of us nowadays depend on the use of a GPS when we travel to places we haven't been before. Those navigational systems are available on our phones and in our automobiles. Type in an address, and a mechanized voice will tell you how to reach your desired destination road-by-road and turn-by-turn.

"Mind mapping" (the process of creating new mental circuits) is much like using a GPS. Wherever you live, imagine that you have taken a new job on the other side of town. The office building is located on a street you've never traveled before and, in fact, have never heard of. On Monday, your first day on the job, you leave early in case you get lost along the way. You carefully type the new address into your GPS. You do not turn on the radio in your car in order to hear clearly each direction that SIRI offers. You seek to eradicate all possible distractions. As you follow the guidance system, every turn is new, every road is previously unexplored, and every landmark you see along the way is unfamiliar. At last, your GPS leads you to your new place of business, and you breathe a sigh of relief. On Tuesday morning, you type the address in again. Now, however, you know that it takes thirty minutes from your front door to your new office, so you don't leave forty-five minutes ahead of time. And you examine places along the route, not only as directional landmarks to be remembered but as spots of interest on their own. There's a lovely neighborhood elementary school. There's a park with walking trails. There's a line of boutiques that may be worth exploring on the weekend. There's a restaurant that you might want to check out. On Wednesday morning, the process is repeated, only now you have the radio tuned to your favorite station. There's no need to worry overly about being distracted. Instead, you want to hear the weather forecast or listen to NPR or rock music. Your GPS is still on, but by Wednesday you no longer pay close attention to it because what was unfamiliar on Monday has become increasingly familiar by mid-week. By Thursday, you no longer type an address in the GPS and you begin to notice additional new things as you drive. By Friday, you could make the trip by rote. What happened? You have created a new mental circuit, a brand new way of thinking about, planning, and implementing travel—a mind map that did not exist on Monday but is now part of your norm.

Our behavioral makeup can be altered by establishing new desired destinations in our internal GPS. If being angry or paranoid or insecure or frightened makes me unhappy, and if I do not like being the sort of person who is governed by those emotions, I have the power to re-direct (to redefine what it means to be me). By refocusing my mental energy on forgiving someone who has offended me, and by practicing that difficult discipline on a daily basis, I can move past the anger that has kept me entrapped in an unhappy place. Psychologists assure us that if we think good things about and express good wishes for people whom we previously judged as being bad, it takes one month for us no longer to be able to hate them. Literally, the capacity for hating that person is removed. And leaving with it, obviously, is the internal misery of carrying a daily burden of resentment. If every day I tell myself that I am worthy, that I am capable, and that I am lovable, in a short time I will have changed my self-understanding from negative to positive. And the beauty of that is that I will then begin to project a new self-image to others who will, in turn, confirm that I am worthy, capable, and lovable. If I write down every night at least one good thing I witnessed, received, or experienced that day, and if I repeat that process night-by-night, and if on the last night of the month I read aloud all the entries from the previous thirty days, I will be transformed from a person who finds life to be unfair or burdensome into a person who finds life celebrative and rewarding. Our brain will make the change for us based on the data we program into it.

If we don't like who we are, we have the capacity to become someone else. The CEO in the hallway may have been victimized by his past. Such is often the case for many of us. Eventually, though, we are challenged either to surrender to what was or to become a new person who is no longer defined by it. We have the option (not only emotionally but, now we are learning, scientifically) to create new mental circuits, to construct new mind maps, to establish new ways of viewing life in general and our own lives in particular, to become a brand new (and happier) version of ourselves. I hope the unhappy CEO will learn those lessons and begin at last not only to discover joy but, also, to spread it around. It can happen for him, just as it can happen for us all.

The Sensitive Student

"Who touched me?" Jesus asked. When they all denied it, Peter said, "Master, the people are crowding and pressing against you." But Jesus said, "Someone touched me; I know that power has gone out from me."

(Luke 8:45-46,

New International Version)

"I just hate to read the newspaper," he said with an unmistakable note of sincerity. "And I try not to watch television, either, until after the evening news is done." We didn't know one another but happened to be seated in chairs beside each other at a local bookstore. I was browsing through a whodunit, considering whether or not to buy. He had read just enough of the morning newspaper to quickly remember why he hated doing so. The front page alone reminded the obviously sensitive young man of how overwhelmed and hopeless he felt in the face of vast issues beyond his control. Apparently he needed to pour out those feelings to somebody. At the moment, I was the only "somebody" nearby.

His was not an unfamiliar emotion. Sadly, though, his spirit of sensitivity too often dulls with age. He said he is a student at Wake Forest University, which is about a five-minute drive from where we now live. In my day, he would doubtless have become a passionate activist, a hippie, someone determined to end war and all of society's isms and put free love in their places. But, these are different days. Some would argue he is smarter than we were at his age. Others would argue he is not smarter, but more cynical.

"Just look at things," he continued. "The Mideast. Nuclear weapons. North Korea. Yemen. Russia. Syria. Iran. Global climate change. Child abuse. Sex trafficking. Homophobia. Gridlock in Washington. Dishonest politicians being rewarded while their critics are demonized. Middle school kids are killing themselves because of bullies. I even have a cousin who attempted it. I mean, this world is just crappy, you know? It's freakin' falling apart. And I have no idea how to fix anything. There's just one of me. So, I feel like

I'm turning into a tortoise or something. I just draw into a shell. When other students on campus talk about issues, I beam out. We can't change anything. It's pointless to think we can."

A few things struck me at that moment. First, he was too young to give up on life. Second, maybe he was going through a personal crisis of which I was unaware, some emotional catalyst behind his assumption that all seemed lost. Third, his sensitivity was impressive. It's too easy at his age, or any age, to become self-absorbed, to lose one's self in the new taste of freedom. You're in college. There are no parents present to chaperone or interfere. You are assumed to be a young adult capable of making moral choices. And, you are free to make those choices in dorms and bars, on spring break and at weekend parties, in inviting clubs with friends and strangers. A hunger for hedonism is easily fed in a plethora of places if that's what you're looking for. But that did not appear to be his hunger. He hungered to do something to make the world better, but the world is just too big. It reminded me of the prayer of St. Brendan: "O God, the sea is so large, and my boat is so small."

Another thing that struck me was the phrase he used and how accurate that phrase often seems: "We can't change things." That, I suppose, is ordinarily true. No one of us can change things. The countless things that are broken in our world, our communities, our corporations, our government, our neighborhoods, and our families are too numerous for any one person to tackle alone. But, if we drop the "s" from the word "things," his statement is no longer valid. Whereas none of us can change everything (all things, plural), each of us can do something to make a positive impact somewhere. We can change something or, at least, be part of the company of committed folks who bring change about. That's what he needed to hear, and what we all need to remember from time to time.

I was first introduced to an old and familiar parable by a dear friend, now many years deceased. It was his favorite story. So, I love it for two reasons: one, because it reminds me of him, and two, because it reminds me of truth. The story goes that it was early morning on the coast. During the night a fierce storm had washed thousands, maybe tens of thousands, of starfish up on shore. There they lay, doomed to die for lack of the ocean water that was their source of life. A little girl walked the shore, picking up one starfish at a time and casting it back into the waters. An older man, having grown skeptical across the years, watched in amusement. Finally he spoke to her.

"Hey, kid. You're wasting your time. You can't save all those starfish."

As she reached toward the sand, picked up another and tossed it into the water, she answered, "Maybe not. But, I can save this one!"

That's the key, the insight needed by that sensitive young man from WFU. That's a lesson he could learn, we all could learn, from a little girl on an early morning beach. We cannot do all things, but we can all do something. And it is not clichéd to suggest that maybe if we all do our something well, there can be a cumulative impact. I cannot cure world hunger. But, I can contribute to a soup kitchen in my community. I can bring canned goods to a food drive in my church, synagogue, school, or civic club. I can send dollars to The Potato Project. I can do something. And so can you. And so can that young disheartened student. If enough of us do even a little, the result can be dramatic, and things can be changed.

Defeatism is sometimes born of the indefensible illusion that I am bigger than I am. That I am assumed to possess larger-than-life powers. That there are unrealistic expectations placed upon me by some external source, whether that be community, family, Deity, whatever. And thus, feeling challenged to fix the world, I begin to take a serious look at how large the world is. In so doing, suddenly I see the vastness of the world's needs vis-à-vis the limited measure of my skills or resources to meet those needs. Overwhelmed by what I see, and convinced that I cannot repair all the damage, I become the tortoise he described. I retreat. I throw up my hands and heart in despair. My word of choice becomes "futile." Why try when I simply cannot do it?

There are those, however, who seem to believe otherwise—those determined little girls who throw one starfish at a time back into the sea, those committed individuals who devote themselves at least to making a dent in the status quo.

A friend of many years is a faithful supporter of Smile Train. Though I do not know a great deal about that organization, I am aware of its mission. They send medical personnel into the poorest countries on the globe and treat children born with cleft palate or other serious facial disfiguring birth defects. Those defects, if left untreated, impair a child's ability to speak and even to eat adequately while physically developing. In some countries, children with such disabilities are denied the privilege of attending school, as their local schools are not equipped to deal with the children's special needs. Thus, not only do those children grow up with inadequate communication abilities and often insufficient nutrition, but also with a sense of rejection and a lack of education. All that virtually ensures for them a future of poverty.

Smile Train goes into those countries and performs surgeries to correct the birth defects and, thus, allows the children who suffered them to have a future endowed with hope. My friend who sends money to that organization often says, "Today I was somewhere on the other side of the world, and I gave a child her smile back." She is aware that over forty thousand children will starve that day. She is aware that even more will be hungry or abused. She is aware that many new babies will come into the world with birth defects that need to be corrected. As a rational person, she is aware she cannot address all those needs. But, as a caring person she is also aware that somewhere that day at least one child got "her smile back." None of us can do all things, but all of us can do something.

Use the word "environmentalism" and you can probably get off unbloodied, just being labeled "a tree hugger." Use the phrase "climate change," however, and you will be challenged by someone who thinks your philosophy about Mother Earth is a direct attack on his philosophy about politics. For most of us, that's not easy to fathom since we all share this planet together. We are all leaving an environment of some sort to our children and theirs. That issue is above and beyond politics. It's about contemporary life *and* the quality of life we long to bequeath to those who follow us. It's not red or blue. There are reasonable places where those who differ on the topic politically can still meet and have a significant impact on those yet to come.

So, what if we took politics out of the equation for a moment? Put on brief hiatus the consideration of how to influence governments around the world to effectively regulate what industries are allowed to do to (or for) our air and water. Those issues must be addressed, but just for a brief moment, look at environmental responsibility/opportunity from a different vantage point. Consider the mindset sometimes seen on bumper stickers: "Think globally, act locally."

If every individual, every household, and every place of business (a) recycled trash, (b) used recycled metal and paper products, and (c) purchased energy-efficient light bulbs and appliances, and if travelers (d) used public transit when available, and (e) opted for gasoline-efficient or electrically-powered automobiles when possible, it is estimated that global climate change would be noticeably reversed (even without a great deal of corporate cooperation). Scientists with expertise in such matters have concluded that simple steps like those just listed would rather quickly reduce the warming effect by 30%. (NASA 2021) In short, individuals can make a difference. It is a matter of choice, not a matter of ability. Perhaps we cannot restore the planet to the pristine nature of Eden, but we can make it cleaner and healthier than it is now. We can take important steps toward leaving our children something fresh, beautiful, and functional. If I do my part and the next person does hers and the next person does his, individual-by-individual, we can change things. That is reality. No one can do everything, but all of us together can do something. And sometimes that something is dramatic.

The sensitive student I met at the bookstore mentioned his cousin who attempted suicide because he was bullied. Such stories are also a sad part of our reality. They are based on the myth that "different" equals "dangerous." To all reasonable people that assumption, obviously, is bizarre. And yet, that does not prevent it from being too widely accepted. Violet actions are usually the result of fear. We do not understand the other, and so we are afraid of them, and motivated by that fear we lash out pre-emptively.

Children and youth are vulnerable and innocent creatures. They assume that others have good intentions and express themselves honestly. They even assume that they themselves are likable and acceptable until someone shatters the illusion. Then, they are apt to fall apart in ways that we adults do, as well, but manage to more effectively disguise. We retreat to anger, sullenness, or chemical abuse, slow methods of putting an end to a meaningful life. The very young are not so subtle, often (and tragically) opting to end life altogether.

We all know of children or teens who have felt judged, rejected, or ridiculed because of their hair color, their body shape, their being differently-abled, their sexuality, their economics, their stutter, their freckles, their neighborhood—factors over which they have no control and which do not determine the quality of any person's essential life or character. Still developing emotionally, they assume that attitudes expressed by others are honest and that, therefore, the problem resides in themselves and their lack of conforming to someone else's understanding of the norm. Such assumptions plunge the young into an abyss of self-doubt and despair.

No one individual can eradicate all judgmentalism and bullying. But, each individual does have the capacity to extend compassion and a sense of community and compassion to persons one at a time. We can comfort. We can encourage. We can include. If young enough, we can sit with someone who otherwise would sit alone in the cafeteria. If older, we can do the same in the lunch or break rooms at work. We can pay compliments. We can extend invitations. We can lend our voices to the increasing chorus of people speaking out against bullying, whether that occurs in person or online. Everyone can do something.

I may not be able to create world peace. But, I can be a proponent and provider of peace in the ways I deal with other people (including those who are not always easy to deal with).

I cannot defeat systemic racism. But, I can treat all persons with dignity and fairness, I can lend my advocacy to local efforts for justice, and I can keep myself open to relationships with anyone whether or not they look precisely like I do.

I cannot overcome someone else's negativity. But, I can remain pleasant to that person, offer a smile (hoping it is sincere enough to be contagious), provide a handshake or hug, acknowledge him or her in a way that says they matter, and know that in so doing that person's life can at least inch in a more positive direction (and my own life will feel more positive, as well). My father used to quote an old hymn or poem. Most of it I do not recall, but these lines have remained in my memory: *Heaven's not gained in a single bound, but by little things piled round on round.*

Two distinct takeaways resulted from my brief encounter with a sensitive student in a bookstore. *[1] Life is imperfect, and wearing rose-colored glasses doesn't help improve what needs to be improved.*

Life happens. Poverty exists, affecting 20% of our nation's public school students. Loneliness exists, affecting 75% of America's adult population. Homelessness is real, with over 600,000 people in our country having no place to sleep tonight. Abuse is real. Trafficking is real. Political corruption is real. Violence is real. Bigotry is real. And none of those issues grow less pronounced or impactful if I pretend they are unreal.

Looking for the positive aspects of life is essential if we are to retain a sense of emotional equilibrium. Life remains more good than it is bad. That in no way denies the reality of the bad. Only people who see that which is good and believe it should be the norm for all others will be energized to undo that which is not good. They recognize that the desired norm is not being achieved, all is not good for all people. Thus, they understand that we have an opportunity (and a moral obligation) to do something to right the ship.

In my own experience, whenever I realistically look at issues that need to be addressed and then take whatever measures I can to address them, that's when I feel better about life in general and my own life in particular. When we take off the blinders … when we see the pains and problems that exist … and when we roll up our sleeves and become part of the solution, then we find senses of meaning and accomplishment that can never be found by living in denial. Do something (if just one helpful thing) every day, and your life will become increasingly positive because you confessed and did battle against that which is negative.

[2] The second takeaway is that self-doubt and skepticism preclude the possibility that my life can make a difference.

The student in the bookstore didn't seem to understand that. Because the problems on the front page were massive, he felt his powers to make a difference were miniscule. The flaw with that kind of logic is that by underestimating his talents, he was overestimating his responsibilities. Who decreed that he ... or you ... or I have to solve all the world's shadowy or alarming issues? Is any one of us that significant in the great scheme of things? None of us possesses the power to fix all that is broken. However, each of us has the power (and the capacity) to help fix some of that which needs to be repaired.

Had he read of children sleeping beneath bridges? Over 100,000 do so every night. And having read that, had he figuratively thrown up his hands in despair? "Who can help that many homeless kids!" What if, however, 100,000 people, reading the same article, had each said, "I can help one of those kids. I can contribute to a homeless shelter. I can join a Habitat build. I can volunteer with a community agency that finds and cares for at-risk children."

Or, maybe he had read of the plight of the aged confined to assisted living. According to the National Center for Health Statistics, there are almost a million and a half senior adults in America who are confined to full time nursing care facilities. Many exist day by day with no outside contact at all, having outlived their acquaintances or having family in faraway places who cannot visit on a regular basis. We read about them and say, "How sad! A million and a half. Who could possibly take on so large a mission!" The other option, of course, is to read about them and say, "I will find one and ease his or her burden of loneliness. I will visit a couple times a month. I will take a flower, a muffin, or a book. I will tell stories or, more importantly, ask to hear his or her stories. I can't help all of them, but I can be a friend and source of comfort to one of them."

We have the power to do something meaningful in the whole world by doing something, however small, in the immediate world that surrounds us. Take on one issue. Make one commitment. Help one person. I may doubt my capacity to repair all things broken, but I should never doubt my capacity to make one bad thing better or one bleak life brighter. And if we all do just that much, the world as we know it can one day be transformed into the world as it ought to be.

A Street Corner Psychic

"I have come that they may have life, and have it to the full."

(John 10:10,
New International Version)

It was a chance thing, unplanned, and more or less impulsive. I had just left a small café in Greenwich Village somewhere near St. Mark's Place. As I walked down a brightly lit street crowded with some people rushing and others strolling, all intent on finding treasures only the Village has to offer, a voice called out to me. "I like your aura."

In all honesty, I've never been one hundred percent certain what an aura is. Is it something only psychics claim to see, like a halo or a spiritual rainbow? Is it an attitude intuitive people can perceive, revealing self-confidence or kindness? Is it a myth altogether, something that exists only on the pages of gothic novels or in the vocabulary of street corner fortune-tellers? Your guess is as good as mine.

"I like your aura."

"Thank you," I answered, pausing for a moment, being in no hurry to go anywhere.

"I'll read your palm for $20. No rush. No commitment to keep coming back for more. It's a deal, sir. And, I can see you're interested."

"How can you see that I'm interested? What makes you think I'm not just amused?"

"For one, you don't appear to be amused. You look kind of sad, if I may be honest. At least, pensive. And second, you stopped when I mentioned your aura. If you weren't interested, you'd be two blocks gone by now. So, what do you think? $20 for a reading?"

I'm not sure I was interested. I think the more accurate word would have been "curious." I've always been intrigued by things paranormal. Spirituality and mysticism are inextricably bound. It's difficult to speak of souls and life beyond this life while summarily dismissing any possibility that there could be those who can somehow help us bridge the gap between worlds. All the world's great religions talk about it. Credible, skeptical journalists across the years have reported the strangest of moments that challenged everything they previously disbelieved. So, I was curious.

I was not, however, convinced. In fact, I was far from it. Down deep, I assume if someone has gifts of seeing and knowing, or gifts of hearing from those we no longer see or know, that person is probably not going to be relegated to a folding chair and small table on a corner in Greenwich Village, selling their wares for $20 a pop. You don't find Jeff Koons doing back alley building graffiti or Beyonce singing on a subway landing for twenty bucks. Still, I was in no hurry. What did I have to lose? It was another out-of-the-ordinary (and, for me, out-of-character) New York experience. And, it was affordable. I reached into my wallet and handed her a twenty.

"Sit down," she ordered softly, pointing at the empty chair across from her. "Show me your palms."

"Both of them?"

"Both of them."

I complied. She held my hands rather tenderly in hers and stared, very silently and for quite a long time. The silence and length of time holding hands with a stranger was becoming somewhat uncomfortable when, as if on cue, she dropped my hands, looked directly into my eyes, and spoke. "Do you want me to tell you what I see, good and bad?"

"Yes."

"You're sure of that? You want me to be honest?"

"Of course. I mean, after I've invested all this capital," I replied with a nervous laugh that apparently fell somewhat short of communicating humor. She smiled in a disarming way. She had seen that reaction before.

"You've got a long lifeline."

"That's a good thing, right?"

"That's a really good thing. It means you're going to live to be an old man. So, you need to make the best of it. But, there's more."

"I'm all ears."

"You help people. You give yourself away for them. You've done it all your life."

"That's good, too, isn't it?"

"To a point, yes," she answered. But she proceeded. "It's just that for some reason you never learned how to ask for help from people. I can sense you want that. You want to be valued, nurtured. You like giving, but you also hunger to receive. There is no balance. You're just not receiving, are you?"

"My wife and kids love me," I countered.

"That's good, but life is a large circle than that. In the larger circle, you don't feel like you're receiving, do you?"

I looked away for a moment, silently considering her words. They did not necessarily reflect some magic on her part, some psychic's way of knowing the unknown about a stranger. Her words were general enough to apply to lots of people, a shot-in-the-dark kind of diagnosis that as often as not would fit just about anybody. Who doesn't want to be valued and nurtured? At the very most, perhaps she was simply a person with Holmes-like powers of observation, well-trained from years of practice. Even so, she touched a nerve that I ordinarily attempted to keep safely bandaged. Finally, I just shook my head, affirming her words and replied, "That's kind of accurate."

"You realize, of course, that no one will figure out what you need unless you tell them. You're smart enough to get that, aren't you? You long to be vulnerable with some even as they are with you, to receive as much as you give, but you don't tell anyone that. So you've established a pattern of giving and allowing others to think that is your role. Why is it so hard to let people know what you need from them?"

"I think it goes back to my childhood. It's a long story, but I've frequently been in a position of caregiving."

"Here's what you fail to see. You are receiving without knowing it. There are people close who are watching after you." With that she crossed a line from the rational to the paranormal as she began to speak of unseen presences from the Spirit World, who she claimed were hovering close. Watching. Encouraging. Guiding.

"Name three," I laughed. Again, it appeared she found my attempt at humor to be less than convincing.

"The very number I see," she answered. "That is not an accident. Two of those watching over you are your parents. They remain very close to you. They're proud of you, by the way." It was a street corner encounter with a psychic in Greenwich Village, a twenty-dollar palm reading. It is safe to guess that a man of my age probably has deceased parents. I didn't see anything particularly clairvoyant about what she said. Still, her unexpected words touched me at a very deep level. "You long to be vulnerable," she had said only moments earlier. And suddenly I was.

Pausing for a moment to corral my emotions and to phrase them appropriately, I replied: "You know, I've always feared that they were disappointed in me. I miss them a lot."

"Disappointed?" she responded with both volume and energy. "No, not for a moment! They are so proud of you. Your mother is sending me that message right now. And your father is nodding. They are close to you. They're watching over you … and also watching over your children." Again, I discerned no need for psychic power in that statement. It was easy to tell that I had loved my parents. Thus, it would be easy to reply with a statement she knew I would want to hear. Probably she had been plying her craft long enough to have a cache of those statements on hand and the experience to know when to use them. Still, they were the right words at the right time for me. "They're watching over you … and your children." I had not told her that I have children. Again, it could easily have been no more than a safe guess. Nothing she had said required special knowledge, I suppose. All that would have been required was to be aware of the laws of probability and to venture some statements based on them.

"There's another presence, too. Angelic."

"Like a guardian angel? I've never really believed in those things."

"It doesn't matter whether or not you believe. You have one. He's helping you make it through this life, and sometimes, friend, you give him some challenges. But he is powerful, and he has a plan. You just need to be open and let it happen."

Once more, I was dubious. The whole Guardian Angel thing has never made sense to me. If it is true, how do you explain the plethora of misfortunes we see for some folks on a daily basis? If those guardians exist, at the very least it would make you wonder if some are asleep on the job. She, however, had announced right up front that my belief or disbelief was not the issue. "It doesn't matter whether or not you believe ... he is powerful, and he has a plan."

"What's the plan?"

"The plan is for you to become truly happy. Happiness is the plan for you. You're successful, but your angel wants more. You're out of balance."

"I'm not sure I'm following you."

"That's because you haven't made room for that concept. It's a road you've never traveled. You like to stay where it's safe, on roads you understand. You stay on roads of serving others, which you do well. And sometimes you inch down a road of self-pity because others are not perceiving or responding to your needs— even though you don't tell them. That sort of road always leads to places you don't need to be, like loneliness and fear and anger and powerlessness. Those watching over you want better for you than that, but you've got to want it, too."

"You'd make a good therapist or preacher."

"This is my road. Let me see your palms again." I extended them, no longer uncomfortable to do so. Briefly this time she looked intensely as she held my hands in hers. Then she gently released me and said: "I have a message. Take it or leave it."

"Let me hear it."

"Happiness is out there for you. Your angel will not give up on that. And your parents won't, either. It's out there for you. But, you have to help."

"How do I do that?"

"Two things. Do not be bound by what you have done or what people expect you to do. And, this is harder, if you want to be loved, it has to start with you. That's the bold message. You know about love and teach others about it, you just don't love yourself enough. There is so much happiness out there, and you will find it. But not until you learn to love yourself."

The next smile on her face communicated without words that the session was over. Even I am intuitive enough to pick up on those signals.

"I'm here if you want to talk some more. I'm easy to find. I even have a website. Got to keep up with the times."

Standing, I looked at the small, kind lady with the European accent.

"You believe in this, don't you?"

"How could I not? I see evidences all the time. Like I said, I like your aura. It's kind and loving. You didn't make that up yourself, you know. Now, go find the kind of life you try to give to everyone else."

For the ensuing years that I lived in that city, I was tempted to return to her corner. But, for what purpose? I am not certain she could have improved on the advice she offered, advice that most of us need to hear whether or not we have confidence in psychics. I'm still not a believer. But, I am convinced that she shared deep and poignant insights with me, as well as advice that has the potential to help me "find life," as she phrased it.

The street corner psychic provided two brief takeaways that have stayed with me and, for those who want a life that is balanced and whole, should stay with us all. *[1] There are those who stand ready to help us, to nurture us, and to love us. But we have to be willing to ask them*. People really are better than they are bad, kinder than they are cruel, and more eager to help than they are to hurt. We allow the news, politicians, and social media to delude us into thinking otherwise, into believing that we are enemies of one another. But most people—even those who do not think like we do or look like we do or dress like we do or vote like we do or worship like we do or live where we do or spend their time like we do—would step forward in a moment of need to help us if needed, even as we would to help them. The critical point, of course, is simply this: How will anyone know we need their help, their listening ear, their kindness, their presence, unless we tell them? Unless we ask them? Someone is nearby at this moment, willing to be the shoulder you can cry on or lean on if you need such. But that shoulder cannot be yours unless you summon up the courage to confess that you need it.

[2] Love has to begin with ourselves. It should never end there, of course. That would be narcissism. But it has to begin there. Self-

acceptance should always give birth to the acceptance of others, just as they are (which is how we want them to accept us). But how can I accept you if in my own life I have no idea what acceptance feels like? Self-forgiveness, if it's real, should always create a forgiving heart that knows what a burden it is for a person to carry a weight of guilt (or for us to carry a weight of resentment). But how can I forgive you if in the depths of my personal existence I have never learned what forgiveness feels like? And so, self-love should always teach us how to love anyone and everyone who crosses our paths (which leads to a life of joy that can be discovered in no other way). But how can I love you if in my own heart of hearts I have not been open to love? How can I give away what I have never allowed myself to receive?

There is something interesting about those of us who lean in the direction of being codependent. We think we can secure happiness only by making others happy. To be sure, that is one of the many methods for finding our bliss. But if we conceive of it as the only method, at best, it becomes exhausting. At worst, it completely misses the point. The point may be that happiness begins at home … that we must learn, as the street corner psychic advised, to love ourselves, to be at home in our own skins, and only then, when we discover personal peace, will we be equipped to make others happy. "You lack balance," she told me. I'm not sure one has to be clairvoyant to understand that. But certainly, one has to be wise.

The Denver Driver

"Sir, did you not sow good seed in your field? How, then, has it weeds?"

(Matthew 13:27,

Revised Standard Version)

My driver in Denver was a local native and as proud of his city as any person can be. Wherever we went, he pointed out places of beauty and importance. Often while explaining their significance to the city (and obviously to him), he would say, "I don't know of another place that has anything like that. I tell you, this city is just about perfect!"

He had just made that remark as we drove from the hotel to the civic center. I don't recall what we had passed, but once again, he had pointed it out with enthusiastic pride, and then again he had sung his familiar refrain: "I don't know of another place that has anything like that. I tell you, this city is just about perfect!" No sooner were the words out of his mouth than we turned a corner and spotted a red brick building on our right. The gaudy signs flashed out the product being sold inside: "Adult Book Store." I said nothing, not wanting to dampen his enthusiasm for all things Denver. But he spoke up, his enthusiasm clearly not dampened by the ugly store across the street. "Okay," he said, "maybe it's not perfect. But, it's about as close as you're gonna get!"

I liked his spirit. And I like the wisdom inherent in his words. Consider two takeaways from what that driver said.

[1] Life is not perfect. People are not perfect. Places are not perfect. The mortal journey is not perfect. If our happiness is contingent on waiting for perfection to arrive, we will be forever waiting and never happy.

A story appeared in the news a few years ago about a British man and woman who were engaged for forty-seven years. After that lengthy span of time, the man died. His fiancé was asked why anyone would delay the wedding for such a duration that is unheard of. She answered, "We didn't want to rush into a marriage until we were sure everything was right." Well, if you can't be sure in forty-seven years of checking it out, maybe your interpretation of the phrase "everything was right," is a bit too demanding. Perfection is not something we're likely to find in this world.

I've never known a person who didn't have flaws, failings, and Achilles heels if we desire to find them. Nor have I ever looked in the mirror without seeing that sort of person looking back at me. At our very best, we are all simply human. There is goodness in that, but there are also chips, stains, and cracks in the porcelain. Sometimes, in fact, that's what makes a piece of pottery all the more interesting. It looks real. So should we.

If I wait to establish friendships only with people who have no flaws, I will never know a friend. If I wait for a job that brings no challenges, I will never have a profession. If I wait for my own life to become perfect before moving in the direction of a fulfilling future, I will never be fulfilled.

Recently, I sat with a young woman who tearfully related mistakes she had made in her relatively short life to this point. "I have messed up so many times," she said.

I simply answered, "Then let each memory be a classroom. Every time you have 'messed up' carries within it a unique learning opportunity to equip you for future successes. It's your choice. You can either be imprisoned or educated by your memories."

I walked a mile with Pleasure;

She chatted all the way;

But I was none the wiser

For all she had to say.

I walked a mile with Sorrow,

And ne'er a word said she;

But, oh! The things I learned from her

When sadness walked with me.

(I Walked a Mile With Pleasure
by Robert Browning Hamilton)

Substitute other words. "I walked a mile with *success*" vis-a-vis "I walked a mile with *disappointment*." "I walked a mile with *joviality*" vis-a-vis "I walked a mile with *hurt*." "I walked a mile with *confidence*" vis-a-vis "I walked a mile with *doubt*." "I walked a mile with *self-assuredness*" vis-a-vis "I walked a mile with *guilt*." Often, as the poem suggests, it is through the less-than-perfect experiences of our lives that our greatest and most lasting lessons are learned. In the simple (though rarely easy) realm of human relations, our most important accomplishment is often learning how to love others as they are rather than as we want them to be. If we are able to pull that one off, then it opens the door for reciprocation—for them to love us as we are. Once that happens mutually, the gift of enduring friendship is made possible. Some of our greatest lessons and most important discoveries come by realizing that people are mortal and must be accepted as such, flaws and all. Life is not perfect. If we wait for it to become so, we will be waiting an awfully long time.

[2] Life is good, in spite of its imperfections. When people tell me how bad life is (and I try to remain sensitive to the fact that in their particular moment, they are probably being honest), I usually ask them to write a "What If?" list. That is a list that begins with "What if I did not have..." and articulates things in a person's life without which their life would be poorer and emptier. If thoughtful and honest, most can come up with a rather impressive litany of beauties and blessings. Then I simply advise them that what they have just composed could be the beginning of a "Because Of" list—a collection of people, events, possessions, opportunities, memories, and dreams that make their lives meaningful and hopeful. Life is essentially good "Because Of" the things on this list. Call it what you will. "What If?" "Because

Of." The point is that all the things on the list exist even in the midst of life's imperfections or momentary challenges and setbacks.

After a speaking engagement at a maximum security penitentiary, I chatted with numerous inmates who attended that evening's function. One by one, they were men who had committed felonies, many of them violent crimes. Some would be released soon. Others were serving long sentences that would keep them in prison until an age when most people would be retired. A handful were serving life sentences and hanging onto slim threads of hope that perhaps someday a Parole Board would be willing to reconsider. That night, after they heard my message, I listened to their stories.

The men in the room had been transformed. Each of them had a spiritual reawakening while behind bars and together had formed a "house church." Several described to me what they called their "conversion experiences." One had begun writing his memoirs in the hope that it might shed light on (and, therefore, improve) the realities of the penal system. More than one had begun to develop a life plan that involved returning to their hometowns and neighborhoods in an attempt to become moral influences to young people. Some had begun to express themselves through writing fiction, poetry, or scripts. One had discovered that he was a talented artist and was creating landscapes on canvas, drawings of open, free spaces in bold colors that were produced behind the drab, gray walls of incarceration. There was a softness to the men I met that night, a gentle spirit I hadn't expected to find in convicted felons. There was humor, laughter, and smiles. An intellectual appetite was obvious, revealed through their words, "Your speech made me think of..." or "Tell me more about what you meant when you said..."

None of the men with whom I conversed that night was living in an environment anyone would desire. There was nothing easy about their home-behind-walls. There were hardships, limitations, and occasionally even dangers. They all recognized and confessed that and did not exist in a state of denial. Instead, they had chosen to embrace the opportunities for personal growth and joy that always exist in the midst of imperfection.

Consider a quadriplegic who learns to paint by holding the brush between her teeth or who plays basketball from his wheelchair. Or the victim of crime who advocates for other victims and, in so doing, harvests meaning and victory from her wounds. Or the person who has lost a career or a loved one and dedicates himself or herself to comforting others who experience loss. A friend of mine, a brilliant endocrinologist, grew up suffering from Type 1 diabetes and, because of that, has dedicated himself to treating others who live with the same disease. The extraordinarily successful career of another friend, one of the kindest and most competent counselors I know, emerged from her own history of abuse as a child.

What are the common threads binding each of those stories (and countless others like them) together? The first is that individuals who achieve almost always do so in spite of challenges and roadblocks. Ours is not a perfect world, but it is also not one that has the power to hold anyone forever captive in darkness so long as we believe in and strive for light. You can move from where you are to where you long to be.

The second common thread is that those individuals who began to craft new futures for themselves came to an understanding that life is good not because of an absence of imperfection but in spite of its presence. Ours is not a perfect world. Even so, there is still goodness out there. And joy. And purpose. And opportunity. And fresh starts. And dreams to chase. And hopes to be fulfilled. And love to express and to receive. It boils down to the "glass half-empty or half-full" cliché. How do we perceive life as it essentially is? What do we desire for our own lives? And, what are we going to do about it?

The raw ugliness of life unexpectedly showed up in a red brick building with a gaudy sign: "Adult Book Store." It flashed its on-and-off resignation to how broken life can be. It implied the loneliness of those who seek whatever they are emotionally seeking in places like those. The emptiness. The sins of abuse or trafficking. The dirtiness that settles like volcanic ash on the souls of those who surrender to that Isle of Sirens. It was all pathos and shadows and a glimpse of the frightening underbelly of life that has lost both hope and noble vision. However, acknowledging that raw ugliness, my driver refused to surrender to it. It was merely a small blemish on the face of beauty he perceived his city to be. He was not willing to let that blemish define the hometown he loved or obscure its myriad virtues. "Okay," he said, referring to the city he cherished," maybe it's not perfect. But, it's about as close as you're gonna' get!"

Life is not perfect. But, in spite of that, it is still good and filled with the potential for transformation, meaning, and joy. Our task is to find that which is good and hopeful and let those things become our greater realities.

A Word of Hope on
a Street Corner in Harlem

"But they who wait for the Lord shall renew their strength; they shall mount up with wings like eagles; they shall run and not be weary; they shall walk and not faint."

(Isaiah 40:31,

Revised Standard Version)

I had just preached at an afternoon community event held in a historic church in Harlem. It was a special event that attracted a huge crowd and several neighborhood choirs that lifted everyone's spirits. I had been invited because I was serving back then as Pastor of Marble Collegiate Church in NYC (known as "America's home of positive thinking"—the church Norman Vincent Peale served when he wrote *The Power of Positive Thinking*). It was a beautiful and busy autumn Sunday. People were everywhere on the grounds of a city park just beyond the church building, involved in all the sorts of activities that beckon when the air is fresh and the sun is shining. Inside the church, I had talked to people about hope *and* justice, honesty *and* maintaining a positive outlook. But, in truth, I was not feeling positive at all. Instead, I was feeling tired and burdened by a hundred nagging worries that fatigue had tricked me into fearing I could not resolve. So, I stood on a street corner, waiting for the light to change so I could walk to the subway and go home. My eyes were as downcast as my spirit felt. Suddenly, out of the crowd, a young man approached. He literally passed by dozens of others and came straight to me. We were not acquainted. A stranger approached another stranger and said, "Don't worry, sir. Everything is going to be just fine." Then he disappeared into the crowd as quickly as he had arrived.

He left behind certain questions in his wake. The first question that confronted me before the light even changed was, "How did he know?" What made him pick me out of the crowd as the recipient of his word of comfort and encouragement? There were certainly more than enough potential prospects for his brand of motivational speaking in that crowded place on that busy Sunday. He could easily have peddled his word of positive thinking to any of hundreds of people standing nearby. So, why me?

Was it random? Just pick a stranger, any stranger will do, and share that message? "Don't worry. Everything is going to be fine." The odds were in his favor that whoever he chose would need to hear that word. One out of three adults is depressed, they tell us. Three out of four feel lonely. The average person carries around more than their share of grief and guilt, fear and fatigue. Maybe he knew all that and understood that whomever he randomly selected would need to hear what he had to say. Maybe he was a Good Samaritan who understood that almost everybody is wounded and lying in an emotional ditch of some sort. Perhaps that day, I was no more than the luck of the draw. And maybe he disappeared to the next corner and shared the same message with somebody else.

Or, was there some other reason he chose me in particular? Was there something written on my face, some message of despair or desperation? And was he sensitive enough to notice what most others would fail to see?

I've seen it on faces. So have you. There are looks of concern or inner weariness that occasionally work their ways to the surface.

Sometimes we wear our emotions not so much on our sleeves as in our eyes. Maybe such was the case for me that day. I wasn't wrestling with one worry but rather with a myriad of them. Family things. Financial things. Physical things. Professional things. I try not to be a fixer because rarely are we able to pull that off. Nonetheless, moments come when we still wish we could fix what is broken in our own lives or the lives of those we love. I was reviewing my 'Wish List' in my own wish-I-could-fix-it moment. Maybe it was more apparent than I imagined. And maybe he was astute enough, aware enough, and kind enough to notice. "Don't worry, sir. Everything is going to be just fine."

His prediction was accurate, of course. Usually in most situations, everything does work out fine. Not always in every situation, but most times in most situations it does. It's just the way life is constructed. Time itself takes care of that. What seems urgent today is forgotten next week, whether or not I resolved it today. That does not mean, of course, that I should ignore pressing issues. It is rather to say that I should not fixate on or be immobilized by them. Years ago I knew a wise woman who would advise her children in their moments of temporary crises: "It will get better, or it will get over." Ordinarily, that's how life works.

In retrospect, I wonder if I listened to his words that day. I know I reflected on them, especially wondering why he chose me and how did he know what I needed to hear? But, beyond those self-absorbed ponderings, did I actually listen? Did I catch the takeaways? The first was the message that *[1] Life has a way of untying its own knots if we are patient and trusting enough to allow that to happen*. My problem too often is that I long to rush from pain to resolution, circumventing the journey between Points A and B. That desire is natural but also ill-advised because of the truth of the second takeaway, that *[2] Many of life's greatest lessons are learned from the stresses or sorrows we experience. Avoid the pains, miss the lessons*.

My father was always my hero. In my mind, he was the wisest man I ever knew. Much of his wisdom was accumulated by being a voracious reader. Much was accumulated by simply having lived long enough to figure things out. As a young adult, I wanted life to be different, better, more fairy tale than day-to-day grind. Thus, I had the habit of complaining about how things were and fantasizing about how I felt they ought to be. Dad would simply advise,

"You've got to play the ball where it lies." It was a golf reference.

In golf, if you hit a shot that doesn't land where you desired, you can't pick the ball up and move it to a better place. You are not allowed to carry it out of the woods onto the fairway or out of the trap onto the green. You have to play the ball where it lies. In so doing, you learn skills and nuances of golfing that cannot be learned if every shot lands on a tuft of grass perfectly positioned for the next swing. Think of Tiger or Sorenstam or Scottie. They've made a fortune by finding creative and skillful ways to play the ball where it lies.

I can't recall the variety of issues I was wrestling with on that autumn Sunday afternoon as I stood on a street corner in Harlem. But, if they were financial, I probably learned from them certain helpful strategies for managing my resources in the future. If they were physical, I probably was motivated to walk a little more, eat a little less, and pay additional attention to self-care in the future. If they were relational, I probably reflected more seriously on my role in making friendships or family connections work. Play the ball where it lies.

And, obviously, as I write this, I realize that the world did not end that afternoon. The sky did not collapse around me. All good things did not suddenly dissipate into an abyss. My angst was momentary. "It will get better, or it will get over." I couldn't sense it at the moment as I stood on that street corner. But a young man passing by apparently knew that I needed to be reminded of one of life's most important truths. In one way or another, sooner or later, his words are almost always correct: "Don't worry, sir. Everything is going to be just fine."

Do You Have Time
To View My Photos?

"You obey the law of Christ when you offer each other a helping hand."

(Galatians 6:2,

Contemporary English Version)

The first time I met her was on a windy autumn morning as I walked west on a street in Murray Hill. It was one of those days when we defiantly cling to the last remnants of warm weather. Cold enough to justify something warm and wooly, many of us were saying our last defiant "No" to the approaching cold. Therefore, I was wearing a plaid sports jacket and navy pants with an open-collared shirt, refusing to confess that I should have worn an overcoat. There she came, an aged woman with a cane, someone I had never met before, who was smiling at me as if we were old friends. Her eyes sparkled with delight when I smiled back and uttered, "Nice morning, isn't it?" She didn't answer my question, no doubt realizing it was rhetorical and more polite than friendly. Instead, she cut to the chase and said in a clipped British accent, "You need a hankie."

Not quite sure what to make of her nor how to reply, I simply smiled and said, "I probably need a stylist." She slowly walked into my space, her body language refusing to confess that anyone owned a space that was inaccessible to another. Lightly touching my coat pocket, she said, "If you're going to wear a jacket this lovely, you need a hankie. One that matches."

Opening my coat, I showed her the tie I carried in an inside pocket. It had been carefully chosen to match the coat and would be put in place only after arriving at the office. Again, ignoring the commonly accepted protocol of not invading another's space, she reached into my pocket (uninvited, of course), pulled out the tie, and attempted to slide it into the handkerchief pocket on the outside of the coat. That particular pocket was still stitched shut. I don't use "hankies."

"Look at you!" she said with, I felt, a bit too much volume. "You're not even prepared to complete your attire. How long have you owned this coat?"

"I don't know really. Maybe two years. Maybe five." Suddenly I felt a bit like a fashion failure being interrogated by a district attorney employed by Ralph Lauren.

"Five years and you've never put a hankie in that pocket?" With that she began to lecture me about the fine details of a properly nuanced appearance.

From time to time along that route, at that same hour of day, we would pass. Occasionally, she would ask if I had gone to Bloomingdales or Lord and Taylor to purchase a hankie. Sometimes, she would describe the bitterly cold air as "refreshment to our lungs." Other times, she would talk about how quickly she heals and how much easier it was to walk after her double hip replacements. She asked about my family, my work, my roots. The encounters were never long. Aside from her positive remarks about her progress following surgery (and how surely she would soon be rid of "this bloody cane") she never made herself the topic. Always it was me, or the city, or the world, or some stranger whom she had just assisted.

One of her projects was to find subway tickets with currency still available on them and give them to folks who appeared to be down and out. From her reports, she has an uncanny ability to find such. One morning, she reported having discovered MTA cards totaling over twenty unused dollars and how, only two blocks back, she had shared them with a person who did not possess sufficient funds to travel from one spot to another in that large and rapid-paced city. She beamed as she told me of assisting an individual whom she had never met before and, in all likelihood, would never meet again. "Do you travel by bus or subway?" I asked. She answered: "Neither. It's too expensive. I always walk. You meet the nicest people that way." It was too expensive for her to take a bus or train, but she gave away tickets to other people who needed those methods of transportation.

I'm not certain what changed on a morning in May when I turned the corner onto Third Avenue and saw her approaching. Her "bloody cane" was still in hand, though she claimed it was primarily because she had gotten used to it and just liked the feel of a walking stick. "My hips are practically healed," she assured me. "I have no pain at all. And I can walk from one side of this city to the other, if I want." Her smile was still warm and engaging. Her clothes, though neat, showed many miles of wear. Nothing had visibly changed, but the encounter was different from any of those that had preceded it.

"Do you have time to view my photos?" she asked. I realized it was the first time she had ever allowed herself to be the topic. Despite our several casual conversations up to that time, I didn't even know her name (though she had made a point to learn so very much about me).

"You have photos?"

Reaching into an old, cloth shopping bag, she produced a small photo album. It was dog-eared, obviously the result of years and years of fondly turning pages. "I carry these with me everywhere," she said. "I just so rarely meet anyone who is interested." I was stung by a sudden sense of guilt that I had never really expressed interest in her story, not even enough to know her name. But, I was relieved to realize she apparently thought I had been interested and that our casual friendship had not been so decidedly one-sided.

"I would love to see them. Please show me."

She opened the book, and my eyes fell upon a beautiful young woman. The woman in the picture was literally spellbinding, with thick autumn hair that surrounded a face that looked like a movie star's. Clearly she had been posed by a professional photographer who had taken the picture for publicity purposes.

"Is that you?"

"It was … once upon a time. I was a dancer. I traveled the world performing, met the most intriguing people, had the most marvelous romances, and even did a stint in Hollywood. But that was long ago."

She continued page by page. There were photos of that stunning young woman, acrobatically posed in what appeared to be impossible positions. One even showed her in ballet attire, balanced on the toes of one foot while holding the other leg straight above her head, pointing into the air. "How does a person do that?" I asked.

"They do that," she chuckled, "while they still have good hips."

On and on they went. Dancing photos. Family photos.

"Do you have family here?" I asked.

"Oh no, they're all gone now. All except for a sister-in-law. But she's not here. She's in California. I would love to see her, but travel is so expensive."

Toward the end of the album were photos of teacups and saucers. "I keep them in my parlor," she told me, "in case I entertain. They are so delicate and lovely. I clean them once a week so they will gleam. Most of them were gifts to me. They come from all over the world.

Aren't they beautiful?" I assured her that they were.

"So, if you clean them once a week," I ventured, "then you must entertain often. I'm sure your guests are impressed by those cups and saucers."

Without a note of sadness, she responded while putting the photo album back into her cloth bag. "I'm not sure anyone has come to tea at my apartment in over ten years. Maybe longer than that. As I said, most of my loved ones are gone now. But, the memories are real. That sort of keeps those loved ones close, I suppose. The cups and saucers are reminders. So, I couldn't imagine not taking proper care of them."

I shouldn't have been surprised. After all, she believed a stranger in a plaid jacket should respect his attire enough to have a hankie in his pocket. Why would she not apply that same sense of respect to her own treasured artifacts, especially when they were more than cups and saucers? They were symbols of friendships once known and still cherished.

She said, "You'll have to come to tea sometime." But, "sometime" rarely arrives, and so our spur-of-the-moment plan for tea never materialized. The last time we bumped into one another, she was on her way to a doctor's appointment. I asked if she was having problems, to which she replied with a smile, "No new ones. I'm not a young dancer anymore. Even with my new hips, walking around this city all the time gets harder to do. And the cold air seems even colder than it used to be. One of these days, I guess I'll have to join my sister-in-law in California. But not yet. We still have to have our tea." That was our final encounter.

Sometime later, I moved from NYC to North Carolina. So, I have no way of knowing where or how my old friend and fashion consultant is. Had the years and the wear on her joints forced her inside, homebound by her physical condition and the winter wind? Had she at last gone west to be near her only remaining family member? Or, did I stop seeing her simply because walking had become too great a chore, and she was forced to use those MTA tickets for her own transportation? Unanswered questions are part of life. I just hope for her sake that the answers were pleasing. I hope they brought friendships. I hope they included people who would knock on her door for a tea party.

In every chance encounter, if we pay attention, there are takeaways, lessons to be learned if we simply take the time to notice them. She taught me several.

[1] Present your best self. "You need a hankie," she announced on our first encounter. Whereas I am no fashionista and am uncertain what wardrobes call for which accessories, to me her lesson had to do with more than mere attire. My best self is one that greets the world with courtesy, civility, and kindness. My best self is accepting and inclusive. It is patient and charitable. It looks people in the eye, shares a smile, asks questions that show them they are being taken seriously. It seeks to help when help is needed. My best self is not bigoted or condescending. It is not arrogant or judgmental. It does not try to re-create people in my own image but rather accepts them in their own reality. My best self knows how to compliment, how to listen, how to laugh, and how to offer comfort or encouragement. "You need a hankie." She taught me always to present my best self to others.

[2] Artifacts are symbols of reality. Her teacups and saucers were no longer of any use to her in a practical way. No one came to call anymore. But she made them gleam every week, polishing them with a sense that bordered on reverence because each one reminded her of someone dear who had given

that piece as a gift. Furthermore, each one reminded her of parties long ago when friends and family would hold those treasures and drink from them while music played in the background and laughter was heard like a piece of music on its own. In her memories, all those who had populated her life in earlier times were with her once again. She inspired me to look through boxes hidden in the attic and to dust off old photo albums that had been unviewed for far too long. Whatever is within them does not simply represent what was. Instead, they are symbols of reality that continue to inform and impact my life through the act of remembering.

[3] Friendships often occur when we orchestrate them. "You need a hankie," she said to a perfect stranger on the streets of New York City. It is doubtful that she cared overly about how I was dressed. Instead, I suspect, it was a method she employed for making contact with others—especially those whose eyes looked back at her when she looked at us and who returned her smile when she offered one. It is so easy to be overlooked as if we are invisible and then to lament the fact that even surrounded by people, we feel alone. One way to address our loneliness is by summoning the courage to make the first move, to speak the first word, to reach out to another, hoping they will reach

back. Some won't. But, others will. And when that happens, the loneliness is diminished. "To have a friend, be a friend," the old cliché goes. It became a cliché because so many find it to be true. When we reach out to others, some will reach back to us.

[4] *A new future exists regardless of our comfort level with the past*. She loved New York. It had been her home for almost eighty years since her parents brought her there from London. It had been her home during the glory years when she traveled all over the world as a professional (and very successful) dancer. When she traveled on the extended and tiring tours, the thought of returning to New York was her source of comfort. It was her home base, the place where she knew she belonged. After all those years, it had to be unsettling to think of moving three thousand miles from "home" to California where her last remaining family member lived. After all, she was no longer a little girl moving to a new place in the safe presence of her parents. And yet, I did not hear a single note of lament when she told me the time was coming when she would make that move. Her past was sacred to her. But that did not preclude a future which could be replete with its own rewards and joys. In short, she was

open to fresh starts and new beginnings. She was open to life.

[5] People need to be seen in order to feel alive. "Do you have time to view my photos?" She carried in her cloth shopping bag a weathered album that contained images of herself—not just her present self, but her life's pilgrimage. But she needed someone to view those photos, to ask about them and remark upon them, in order to validate what the pictures represented. They represented her. And to be seen and acknowledged verifies that a person does not exist merely as a memory or a relic, but as a living being who deserves to be noticed.

There was something else in her question, "Do you have time to view my photos?" or just, "do you have time...?" Essentially, she was asking, "Will you take time for me, make time for me, make room for me? Will you indicate to me that I matter? Am I as important as whatever thing it is that you're rushing to?" As urgent as our next meeting or appointment may be, can it possibly rival the significance of the human being who interrupts our hurriedness? That was a teaching moment of inestimable significance from our first brief encounter on a cold and busy street. Do I allow myself to become too busy to make time for people?

I have no idea what became of her. But, wherever she is, I hope in mind and spirit she is dancing. And, I hope there are frequent breaks for tea with friends.

Hoping To Grow Up

"Young people, enjoy your youth. Be happy while you are still young... You aren't going to be young very long."

(Ecclesiastes 11:9-10,

Good News Translation)

There is a Starbucks just down the road from where I now live in Winston-Salem, North Carolina. It's populated by students from Wake Forest (five minutes away), patrons of the numerous stores in a shopping center across the street, parents who just dropped off their children at a nearby elementary school, and others of us who need an additional shot of caffeine to tackle a new day.

Recently, I bumped into an acquaintance there. We were in grad school together back in the day when people still used rotary phones. Sitting down with our lattes, we chatted about life, love, and longevity. At one point he asked, "What do you want to be when you grow up?" It's a funny question to pose to someone who remembers watching Mickey Mantle play baseball. He intended it that way. His actual question was about what I want to do with the remainder of my life.

I answered, "I'm just hoping to grow up." That's another strange statement from someone my age, but it's true. Growing old is easy. The years fly by at an accelerated pace. You can't slow them down if you try (and, Lord knows, we have created all manners of attempts to do so). Growing up, however, is not as easy as growing old. Growing up involves things like maturity, personal awareness, wisdom, and a sense of being at peace with mystery, self, and the world. None of that means "resignation" or using the all-too-flippant statement of acquiescence, "It is what it is." Instead, it means finding the right place in life.

"How will you know when you're grown?" he asked. I answered, "I'm not sure I will. If I ever arrive, I will have ceased to grow … and maybe I won't have reached 'up' yet." He nodded as only a fellow journeyperson who has been around a while can. There's something dangerous, maybe even deadly, in "arriving" in life.

When I was a student at Duke I used to witness retired professors, advanced in years, who would make daily sojourns to the library with pens and legal pads in hand. I marveled at that (what time I wasn't laughing at it). "Why on earth would anyone study when not required to?" I wondered. Now I know. It's because life is so brief, and there is so much to learn. Everything we learn makes life richer and deeper. When we are no longer interested in discovering what we can about the great mysteries that surround us, at that point we cease to be fully alive.

There's a little jazz club I often frequented in NYC. It has good food and drink, and usually the music is an A+. I developed a friendship with a man who sang there once a week. His name was Tony. When I knew him, Tony was in his early 80s. Many years prior, he had been the lead singer of a doo-wop group called The Willows. They made hit records, but that day had long since passed. Even so, he possessed enough of a repertoire to just do over and over what he used to do back then, knowing full well that an audience would be there. But that's not who Tony was. He continually sought out new music. He kept writing music. He regularly reinterpreted old songs in new ways. His voice, though deeper by an octave or two than it was in his doo-wop days, was still pitch-perfect, and he worked hard to keep it that way. There was something unmistakably young about Tony, even with the number of years he had chalked up. He decided not to stop growing.

I think "grow" is more important than "up." Maybe the journey eclipses the destination. In fact, in almost Thielhardian fashion, it could be that the destination does continue (and should continue) to extend before us no matter how diligently we seek to reach it. I like that. If I reach it, if I decide I know enough and or can do enough or am enough, then I will be old. At that moment, life will lose its sense of adventure. I want to grow up, but with an emphasis on the "grow" part. Thomas Moore caught the essence of that in his book *Ageless Soul* when he wrote: "When I use the word *aging*, I mean becoming more of a person over time. I keep an image in my mind of cheese and wine. Some get better with the simple passage of time." (New York: St. Martin's Press, 2017, p. 5)

What if growing older equals growing wiser? Most of us remember the recklessness of our youth (and even of years long past it). Sometimes, as teens or young adults, we felt we were stretching boundaries that needed to be challenged, jousting at cultural windmills that had too long been honored without reason or moral justification. But those moments were more risky (even courageous) than reckless. At other times the illusion of invincibility led us to do things that sufficient aging protects us from. They were frighteningly reckless.

How many memories come to countless minds about moments behind the wheel of a car or under the influence of alcohol or giving in to unprotected passion or any of numerous other occasions when one gambled with their own safety and security? The results could have been tragic, and for many, they were. But by pure luck, most of us avoided tragedy. Given sufficient years to observe in other lives, what could have happened in one's own equips and inspires a person to make more reasonable choices. Growing older while reflecting on the past equals growing wiser.

Sometimes growing wiser results not from reflecting on near misses, but rather from simply observing the flow of life. That especially refers to developing a historical perspective. In youth and young adulthood, understandably one's primary concern is his or her own story. Where are you going? What will you do? What dreams will you pursue? What measures can you take to help them come true? Who will you marry? Where will you live? But later in life we begin to realize that ours is not the only story. In fact, our story makes more sense only when juxtaposed with others'. To be a good spouse, I need to reflect on the stories of others who were (or were not). The same advice is true for being a good parent. To protect democracy, it is wise to be aware of political trends throughout the centuries when democracies crumbled (and, thus, to become aware of what movements to avoid, protest, or vote against in our current age). To invest wisely, one needs to know the history of a particular company or of the stock market itself. To have a sense of self, one grows inestimably by learning about your ancestry (who made you who you are). The list is practically without limit, but the point is simple: We move forward most productively by occasionally looking back. A sense of history empowers us to make wise and fruitful decisions for the future. It's part of growing wiser.

Certainly, growing older involves gaining experience. And experience comes in no other way than having been around a while. As the Farmers Insurance commercial puts it: "We know a thing or two because we've seen a thing or two." A friend, who is a master carpenter and cabinet designer, was showing me his shop recently. As we walked from one area to the next, he spotted a screwdriver that had dropped to the floor. Slowly he bent over to retrieve it. Doing so was not without effort; it was done slowly and punctuated by puffs and groans. When he straightened back up, he said with a grin, "When I was young, I could've picked that tool up in a nanosecond. Of course," he added, "when I was young, once I picked it up I wouldn't have known what to do with it." His craft has been perfected by aging, by the constant refining of his skills and by amassed wisdom. We know a thing or two… and can do a thing or two… and are really good at a thing or two… because we've lived long enough to see a thing or two. Aging produces experience

I sat at lunch one day with a friend of many years who is a best-selling author. I said to her, "Sometimes I wonder if people are interested in hearing what a guy my age has to say. Maybe I'm no longer relevant." She (who is about my age and whose books continue to hit *The Times* list) answered, "Michael, you and I have a gift that only time can provide—experience." Of course. Age brings that. We've learned what to do with the screwdriver once we pick it up. Age brings knowledge that was often learned the hard way, but still learned. You don't have to speculate or ask, "What if." You know what will happen "if this" or "if that" because you've been there. You know where this road will lead because you've walked it. You learned where the potholes are, as well as where the groove lanes reside. And now you can share that info with others as they are as they are embarking on their own personal life-journey. So, not only does growing up equal growing wiser, it also equals being experienced (which is the source of wisdom that enables us to have a positive impact on others).

There's also this: Growing up sometimes means growing more satisfied. That's not the same as becoming resigned to the way things are when they shouldn't be that way. Instead, it means developing a more complete worldview—one that sees the flowers as well as the weeds. Several years ago, I heard Garrison Keillor on *A Prairie Home Comp*anion say something to the effect that once we quit trying so hard to fix the world, we become a more healing influence within it. I think I understand what he meant. When we lack a sense of thankfulness for the good parts of life, then the bad parts transform us. Much of the news is dominated by persons of passion who are saying things that need to be said. However, some say it with such vitriol that there is a backlash. People become angry at them because they seemingly add fuel to the flames of discord that singe our souls on a daily basis. We long for voices that say: "Our society has imperfections and needs. How can we positively address them in order to repair what is broken and to provide hope, dignity, and compassion to all?" We resist voices that make us feel even worse about things than we did to begin with.

I am thankful for people in the healthcare industry who treat all individuals alike, even those who may have trouble paying their bills. And there are lots of practitioners like that whose stories can inspire and, thus, need to be told. I am thankful for journalists who report the truth in such fashion that the public is properly informed but also, in ways that maintain a spirit of public hope. I am thankful for teachers who keep planting seeds of values in little children, believing that someday those seeds will bear fruit in society at large. I am thankful for employers who do not abuse workers or customers and who also give back to their communities. I am thankful for neighborhood gardeners who provide food to the hungry and for volunteer tutors who provide mentoring to kids and for Habitat for Humanity painters and carpenters who provide homes for the homeless and for readers and musicians who brighten the lives of those confined to nursing care centers and for school nurses and little league coaches and scout leaders and Sunday School teachers and pet shelter workers and for the next-door-neighbor who mows the aged lady's lawn or the woman on the other side who takes her a casserole while she recuperates from surgery. There are so many good people doing good things to create a good world. Their stories need to be told because those stories protect us from a slow slide into cynicism and, more importantly, because they inspire us to do our part to make an often bad world better. They help us learn how to grow—maybe even how to grow "up."

We are still growing, my Starbucks friend and I. We agreed about it that day. Something within us refuses to pause on the journey (i.e., to grow old). Years accumulate, yes, but so does a spirit of appreciation for the new as well as an appetite for adventure as we prepare to face it. So, here's the takeaway my friend and I agreed upon: *"Age" is not a synonym for "over." In many ways, it just positions us for the next chapters of growth.*

"I'm still a kid inside," he said with a grin. About that time an employee, a young lady—about twenty—paused at our table. "Our cashier is new," she said. "I'm just checking to make sure she gave everyone their senior adult discounts." At that, my friend laughed out loud... just like a kid.

Heroes Never Die Here

"Since we are surrounded by so great a cloud of witnesses ...."

(Hebrews 12:1,

English Standard Version)

I wrote this piece in late winter, 2019. My wife and I had just returned from visiting a friend who lives in upstate, New York. During our weekend there, the three of us drove to Cooperstown where for the first time I visited baseball's Hall of Fame. During that visit, I had a brief encounter with a young woman who worked as a clerk at the HOF library. The following (including the takeaway) is what I wrote after returning home to NC. It initially appeared as a blog on my website.

I did something this week I have wanted to do my entire life. I finally made it to Cooperstown, New York, and spent an entire day in the Major League Baseball Hall of Fame. Without a single fear of overstating anything, it was one of the best days in my entire life. Ever. Bar none. To me, it was like standing on holy ground.

My dad was a lifelong Yankees fan, as was his dad before him. I grew up on the stories of Ruth and Gehrig, DiMaggio, Reynolds, Raschi and Lopat. When I was a kid, he took me to see the Yankees play the Senators in the old Griffith Stadium. I saw Yogi Berra and Elston Howard. It was the year of "The Chase for 61." I saw Mantle hit one home run and Maris hit two. This week, those memories came alive when I stood in front of their photos, when I looked at some of their equipment and uniforms, and when I read again of their legacies.

My mom's first cousin was a man named Jake Early. He played eight years for the Washington Senators and one more for the St. Louis Browns. One year, he was the starting catcher for the American League All-Star team. So, I went to the HOF Library and asked if, by chance, they had anything related to him. Jake never made the HOF but he had a good career, and they keep files on lots of players who were never awarded plaques on the museum's walls. A very gracious young lady working as a librarian answered, "I suspect we have a file on him. Heroes never die here." She disappeared into another room for a few minutes and then emerged with a folder on which was written the words: "Early, Jake."

Though he was my mom's cousin, everyone in the family always called him "Uncle Jake." So I sat at a table and read newspaper clippings about Uncle Jake, his skills, his accomplishments, and his trademark sense of humor. For example, he would do such strange things behind the plate that batters would become distracted and sometimes fail to even swing. Once he sang a country song with such twang and volume that Ted Williams stepped out of the batter's box, bent over, and held his sides while laughing. That was vintage Uncle Jake.

An interesting phenomenon occurred from time to time throughout my day in Cooperstown. Occasionally (and, I never saw it coming) I would be overcome by emotion. I spent most of the afternoon in the Hall of Plaques, not missing a single one. Sometimes I would stand before the plaque of superstars who played in a league for African Americans before they were allowed to play in the Majors, and having read their info I would find myself saying out loud, "Thank you. Thank you for your devotion to the game. I'm sorry for so much of what you experienced, but I am thankful that you paved the way for others who were yet to come. And I am thankful that you used incomparable skills to bring hope and joy to so many who had so little." Or, I would stand before the plaque of a player my dad had told me about (Walter Johnson, Ty Cobb, Satchel Paige, Johnny Mize and others), and my jaw would drop (not figuratively, but literally) as I read their stories.

Occasionally the emotions even brought me to tears. Four times come to mind: In the Hall of Plaques ... in the section on Babe Ruth ... during the movie when watching the segment about how the Chicago Cubs finally won the World Series... and in the library reading through the file on Uncle Jake. Watching the movie made me miss my friend, Alex, who was a lifelong Cubs fan but died just a few weeks too soon to see his beloved team finally win the World Series. While reading plaques and looking at Ruth's memorabilia, I kept wishing my dad were alive to see it with me. And while reading the information about Uncle Jake, I kept wishing my mom were at the table to celebrate her sense of family. With no warning on those occasions, tears came. They were moments I wanted to share with those who would have found them so incredibly meaningful, but those dear ones were gone.

Processing what occurred, I find myself thinking that maybe the emotions came because those dear ones were not gone after all. Maybe I experienced what I did so intensely because they were, in fact, there. With me. Beside me. Even within me. Don't misread. I'm not talking about some ghostly reappearance of anyone. Instead, I'm talking about influence and impact. My dad's sense of the game, my mom's sense of family, and my friend's sense of loyalty to his team made impressions on me that their deaths cannot take away. Every person whom I ever cherished has left something behind, some fingerprint on my soul, that lives on even when they do not. In moments when those influences reemerge, those persons are alive again, powerfully present in my own life.

"Heroes never die here," the young librarian said. That's the takeaway for us, I think. ***Those whom you have loved and lost are, in the final tally, not "lost" at all***. Whatever they were to you, whatever they brought to the table, whatever impact their lives and love had, all that lives on as long as you do. They helped make you whoever and whatever you are. So, today be aware that the best and most essential parts of the ones you loved will remain with you always.

In Cooperstown I was surrounded by the wonderful stories of all the faces on all the plaques and films and yellowed pieces of newsprint. Those heroes were for that day magically present in a museum that, for me, became a *Field of Dreams.* (a film by Phil Alden Robinson, 1989, 20th Century Fox) And others were there, too — people who maybe never even visited Cooperstown but who inspired my love of the game and whose memories grow richer with time. In ways too mysterious to be defined and too real to be denied, you have your own field of dreams, your own circle of influences who not only made you who you are but, in a real sense, continue to do so.

Can You See A Rainbow In This?

"Seek, and ye shall find."

(Matthew 7:7,

King James Version)

"Can you see the rainbow in this?" He was a little kid, not quite yet a youth, on the corner of 28th and Park. There's often a vendor there in the afternoons, selling a magic potion billed as "a rainbow maker." The young buyer was waving the wand and creating huge bubbles. Splashes of color were here and there, the kind soap detergent creates, but the vendor had promised "a rainbow." Inching past the full naivete of childhood, this not-quit-yet-youth on his way to skeptical adulthood apparently wondered if he had been sold an empty promise. He desired a second opinion. "What do you think, mister?" he asked me. "Can you see a rainbow in this?"

In all truthfulness, I did not see a rainbow. Such may occasionally occur via bubble-makers, but not that day. Maybe it was because I was in a hurry. Maybe it was because I had long since ceased to look for rainbows in dish detergent. For whatever reason, I didn't see what he was inquiring about. There were, however, a variety of colors in intriguing patterns. So, I lied. It was a white lie, a kind lie, a lie not yet perceptible to a child his age but quickly discernible to the other adults on the corner. "You know, I do think I see a rainbow in some of those bubbles. You have to look from the right angle, but yes, I think I see a rainbow."

The child in him took over. "Yeah, me, too. If I wave it slow enough and the bubble comes out just right, it makes a rainbow. I don't see many rainbows usually, but this thing will make them."

The light changed. I crossed toward the subway entrance, and he remained on the corner, still in pursuit of the perfect bubble.

I like the fact that the child in him saw a rainbow where most of us could not. Physically, as he confessed, he doesn't see many rainbows usually. In the city, unless one lives on the East River or the Hudson, or on the northern-most or southern-most tips of the island, rainbows are hard to spot. The open sky itself is hard to spot.

When you look up, for the most part you see high-rise buildings, monuments of concrete, powerfully and often beautifully architectured, but blocking out most of the sky. No visible sky = no chance of spotting rainbows. The boy, however, was determined to create his own. Even when the vendor sold him no more than a dream, the child still saw what his heart longed for. There was something imaginative, fresh, irrepressible, and innocent in his stubborn optimism. "If I wave it slow enough and the bubble comes out just right, it makes a rainbow. I don't see many rainbows usually, but this thing will make them."

In life we often have to find rainbows others cannot see. There's really no Shangri La, no place where Pollyana can confirm her worldview. All too often, the children on the street corners pass silently into adolescence and then adulthood, seeing just enough dirt and grime that they become like the rest of us adults and sadly forget how to look for rainbows or even how to believe that they exist. They surrender the power to see rainbows that are actually there for those who keep their eyes and their minds open.

It's really a lot like Yes, Virginia, There is a Santa Claus. (editorial by Francis Pharcellus Church, NY, NY: The Sun newspaper, 1897) It's like believing in unicorns and elves and guardian angels. There's a spirit in most of us that needs to be somehow kept young or else the best part of us grows tired and suspicious. Most of the time, I suspect, rainbows only appear to those who expect to see them.

Today I was recalling things my children did and said when they were very small. Those were the days when they thought mommy and daddy were heroes and the world was an adventure. Among the cherished memories that I relived today was one of pulling into the driveway when my older son was just a toddler. He was behind me, carefully fastened in his car seat. As we turned from the road onto the asphalt path toward the carport, I was suddenly aware of how derelict I had been in my duties as a yardkeeper. The grass was crying out to be mowed. Weeds alongside the driveway were at least four inches in height and had literally begun to bloom. Seeing that, I muttered beneath my breath, "Stupid weeds!" No sooner had those words been whispered (literally, no sooner than they crossed my lips), than I heard a beautiful little voice from a car seat say, "Daddy, look at the pretty purple flowers!" I had seen weeds. He, however, had seen blossoms.

"If I wave it slow enough and the bubble comes out just right," the boy on the corner said, "it makes a rainbow. I don't see many rainbows usually, but this thing will make them."

Maybe I fail to see rainbows or pretty purple flowers because I no longer believe they are there. We grow old and cynical. Or is it the opposite? We grow cynical, and that makes us old. Either way, it's not that rainbows and pretty purple flowers cease to exist. It is rather that we've seen enough dirty skyscrapers and summer weeds that we no longer look for beauty in the midst of it all.

There's an adage that I need to remember more frequently than I do. I probably ought to paint it on the dash of my car, have it made into a refrigerator magnet, or tattoo it on my arm so that I will see it daily and not forget."In life, we ordinarily find what we choose to look for." It really is true, you know.

Social media, the evening news, and partisan politicians seeking personal gain deceive us into believing that there are no rainbows or purple flowers. They infuse us with skepticism and fear, making us assume the worst about others, and causing us to view those who are "different from" us as being "threats to" us. At what point did "different" become synonymous with "dangerous"?

Advertisements convince us that without the proper car or clothes or jewelry or body sculpting or hairstyle or river cruise, we are missing something inexpressibly important. I recall the unparalleled joy of spending Saturday afternoons with my Dad, culminating in a soda and a chili dog at the Little Castle Grill. In those days, it probably set him back $3. There was no fine china at the Little Castle, no wine list, and no caviar. Fortunately, no one told me I was supposed to be disappointed. Therefore, I was thrilled instead.

So, what are the takeaways from my encounter with the street corner rainbow maker?

[1] There are rainbows in life. Remember, that also means there is rain. Life is never all good or all bad. But there is goodness, beauty, and reason for hope. Kind people exist. Laughter exists, as well. Visual splendors of nature exceed anything an expensive art dealer can sell. There is music to be heard, whatever your favorite genre happens to be. Good people still outnumber the bad ones, and they do good things on a daily basis. There are folks who will love us, if we let them. Or who will help us. Or who will stand beside us even if others walk away. There are rainbows in life.

[2] To see rainbows, we have to look for them. Rainbows require what? They require rain. Put another way, pains and problems come. They are unavoidable. Life happens. It serves no purpose to deny the harsh realities of living. However, what else do rainbows require? They require sunlight even while the rain is falling. Life is a mixture of good and bad, high and low, sunshine and shadows, laughter and tears. Sometimes we have to focus on the good parts in spite of other parts that don't feel good at all. In other words, sometimes we have to make the conscious choice to look for the sunlight. In life, we ordinarily find what we choose to look for. Dr. Barbara Frederickson advises: "Visualize your best possible future... Make finding positive meaning your default mental habit." (Positivity, NY, NY: Crown Publishers, 2009, p. 198)

[3] Life is most rewarding when we nurture the child within us. Without acknowledging our inner child and allowing that spirit to dance from time to time, we become tired, captives to routine, bored with things as they are... and, boring to others as we are.

Near our current home is a ballet studio. Sometimes, I drive past it in the late afternoon when classes have just ended. As I sit at the stoplight beside the studio, I see clients on their way out of the building. Apparently, they offer classes, one for children and one for adults. Dancers from one class exit with big smiles, some of them still stepping and twirling as their parents struggle to hold onto their hands. Another class, it appears, is for adults. Out they come, young women mostly in their 20s and 30s, towels draped around their necks, some learning to dance, some sharpening their skills, and others there just for the exercise or camaraderie. As they exited recently, one woman stood out to me. That's because she is, to wager a guess, easily eighty years old. Maybe well past that. She didn't stand quite as straight as some. But neither did she exude the same sense of post-dance (post-workout) fatigue as most of the others. She strode out of the building, like the children, almost still dancing. Her smile was broad and authentic. She may be the youngest of all the women in her dance class, not according to the calendar, but according to the spirit she maintains inside herself.

Children have an inner spirit that recognizes the importance of having fun. Whether that means dancing, using one's imagination in creative ways (like the kids' game, "Let's pretend"), trusting in the fundamental goodness of others (and of life itself), believing in possibilities of things yet to come, reaching out to people to disarm our loneliness (as children do when they ask their best buddy, "Can you come out and play?"), embracing mystery, laughing out loud, allowing a sense of adventure to transcend a fear of embarrassment, or seeing the magic in little things, when we allow the child within us to emerge, we allow the adult within us to find life in its fullness.

The child on the street corner by now has reached his mid-teens. I sometimes wonder what adolescence is making of him. More often, I wonder what the adult influences in his world are making of him as he steadily moves in their direction. Has he realized that there were no rainbows in the soap bubbles? And if so, has he given up on rainbows altogether? If that has happened, then he is not merely growing up. He is, instead, growing old. There's a profound difference. Growing up is to incorporate all the richness of what we have been into what we shall yet become. Growing old is to relinquish that, to forget the beauty and the inherent Truth (with a capital T) of childhood. When that happens, we open ourselves to a host of visitors who can take the life out of living—visitors with names like Cynicism, Fear, Weariness, Routine, and Boredom. I hope he refuses to make those unwanted guests welcome. I hope, instead, that even now and eighty years from now he still believes that rainbows can appear in soap bubbles. For if he believes, he will look for that. And if he looks, that is what he will find.

The Dancer Mom

"Judge not...."

(Matthew 7:1,
King James Version)

While attending an Urban Workers' Conference in Chicago in March, several of us met with city officials, social service caseworkers, sociology instructors, and faith and civic leaders. The windy city was also a frigid one that week, with highs in the 20s and lows so low I didn't want to hear the number.

One evening the members of our groups met one-on-one with people the conference billed as "marginalized." They included at-risk youth, low-income single-parent families, individuals who had trouble finding work because of past legal issues, the unemployed, the working poor, the uninsured, the under-housed, and numerous other categories that took on very human faces as we listened to their stories on that cold Chicago night.

For part of the evening, four of us were asked to interview a young single mom (late 20s, I estimated) who worked as an "exotic dancer" in a club on the city's south side. "Exotic dancer" was merely a polite euphemism for something earthier, in truth, considerably earthier. If her dancing were sufficiently alluring to her almost all-male audience, she could make $500 on a particularly good night. As she reported, those "good" nights felt anything but good when inebriated strangers stuffed bills into her garter.

She seemed suspicious (or, more accurately, "guarded") when she took a seat across from us. Initially, I couldn't understand that. She knew why we were there. We were people who would listen and, hopefully, would compile reports that might enable "the marginalized" to qualify for increased benefits and assistance. Thus, I assumed she (and all the others present) would greet us professionals with smiles and gratitude. It took me a while to figure out that, in her estimation, a man is a man... and her history had taught her that smiles were almost inevitably misinter-preted... and that any "benefit" is ordinarily offered with strings attached. That's how things worked in her world. Why would they be any different from someone else's?

Our conversation with the young woman began politely but clearly at a superficial level. We spoke about the weather, the city, the Cubs and Bears, the beauty of Lake Michigan, and a few dining spots with world-class comfort food that were known only to locals. Then we inched into our purpose for the conversation.

"Tell me what you do," someone said.

She replied, wearing an expression that was not quite but almost a smirk, "You know what I do. It's written in your notes, right?" Obviously, she was right.

"It says 'exotic dancer,'" the man replied. "Tell me what that is."

"As if you don't know. What man your age doesn't know?"

"I'm not from Chicago."

"Oh, sorry. I guess we're the only city on earth that has women who dance for money."

"Would you mind telling us about your job? I interjected"

"I dance on a stage in a place with a deejay, a big bar, expensive drinks, and an audience full of men who have wives at home who mistakenly believe their husbands are at a meeting. Most of those guys also mistakenly believe that they are attractive to women half their age. So, I dance for them. I flirt with them. And they stuff money in my garter belt. The better I dance and the more I flirt and the drunker they get, the more money I take home. Sometimes I laugh at them. But most of the time, I am disgusted by them. That's what I do."

She glared at me, awaiting a response. Probably she thought I would be judgmental or dismissive. I tried, instead, to remain completely professional, as if she had just told me she was a policewoman or an accountant.

"You're young and articulate," I began. "You are obviously very bright. Why do you choose to work as a dancer in the sort of environment you just described, especially if, in your own words, it disgusts you?"

She eyed me for a long, silent moment, trying, I suppose, to determine if my question was clinical or condescending. Finally she responded with a question of her own. "You're not a parent, are you?"

I am a parent. Being such is one of the greatest joys of my life. I'm also a grandparent of two young and precious children. So, I know about the love you feel for your kids and how it is unlike any other love at all. I told her that. She then asked another question.

"If you're a parent, then how can you ask why I do what I do? I'm a mom. My daughter is seven years old. She never knew her dad, and she never will. He was long gone as soon as he found out I was pregnant. She has never received a penny's help from him. I want her to have everything... every single thing that a child can have. She is the best part of my life.

"So, I do what I can to make enough money for us to live where it's safe. We don't live in luxury, that's for sure. But our place is secure. There are nice neighbors around. My daughter's school is a half block down the street, and it's a good school. My grandmother is a ten-minute cab ride from us. She comes over at night and helps my little girl with her homework and puts her to bed. I put food on the table and decent clothes on my child's back. I take her to church, and she's in a scout troop. I'm giving her the life I didn't have—the life she deserves. That's why I do what I do! But you ask me why I do it as if I'm dirty. Well, I'm not dirty. I'm a mom who will do anything because I love my child."

It was not my role to enter into a debate nor to speak in self-defense. It was all of our roles, instead, to give her room to say and feel whatever needed to be said and felt. A woman in our group picked up the questioning.

"I hear you. I know you love your child and endure your job in order to provide for her. But still, why that job? You're young and articulate and obviously bright. You could do something else."

"I could," she answered. "I could do something else. But what would that something be? I dropped out of school in the 11th grade. I can't go back, not now. I've got to take care of my daughter. Without a diploma, what kind of job can I get? I guess I could be a cashier at a grocery store or something. But then I'd make $10 an hour. What kind of neighborhood would I be taking my child to at $10 an hour? What kind of apartment? What kind of school? What kind of life?"

We visitors didn't answer because we didn't have an answer. Chicago was not our city. Her life and ours were incredibly dissimilar. We were there simply to hear stories and pass reports of human needs along. But, there was one thing that mother and I had in common. We both loved our children with a love too deep to adequately put into words, a love so deep that either of us would go to any length necessary to take care of them.

"You're not a parent, are you?" she had asked, assuming that was why it appeared I couldn't wrap my head around the choices she made. But, I am a parent. And because of that, whether or not I fully understood her choices, I did at least fully empathize.

As I think back on that conversation with the dancer mom, there are three takeaways that seem clear.

[1] Sometimes we do what we have to do in order to survive. Parents know this. Soldiers know this. Employees in difficult (and sometimes dangerous) professions know this. Women wearing hard hats know this. Men in hazmat garb know this. In too many situations, spouses know this. In all probability, you know this from some personal experience in times past.

The dancer-mom didn't want to dance. But she did want to adequately provide for her child. At that crossroad, she couldn't discern many attractive options. So she did what she believed she had to do in order to survive the predicament in which she found her family.

An acquaintance who is a firefighter confessed to me that more than he hates anything at all, he hates the safety classes he is required to take annually in order to remain certified for his job. He said he almost always feels more experienced and more qualified than the ones who teach. He rarely learns anything he didn't already know. Sometimes the classes are out of town, and he is forced to travel and be away from home. "But," he said, "as I much as I dread it when those classes roll around, I also understand why we have to take them. Ours is a dangerous job, and we have to know what to do in order to survive."

Unfortunately, there are moments in life when people make choices they would prefer not to make. But when the choices are made, they simply try to do whatever they must in order to survive. I need to remember that before I am too hasty in passing judgment.

[2] Always listen to helpful critique. But, do not accept harmful criticism.

Most of the time, those who offer counsel do so because they have our best interests at heart. The counsel may not be wise or appropriate for us, but it is rarely malevolent.

My mother used to say, "I never tell you anything that isn't born of love." It didn't always feel that way when her words sounded strict or when they were at cross-purposes with my youthful own wishes. But looking back, I know her words were true. Later on, I did the same thing with my children. We all do. "Don't ride your tricycle in the street." "Don't wander off with strangers." "Don't play with fire." "Don't jump in the deep end of the pool." There are moments when those commands will sound confining and overbearing to any child. But, they are born of love. So, to the extent possible, always try to be gracious with your critics. "You're not a parent, are you?" the dancer-mom asked me. I suspect she was making a kind allowance for what seemed my lack of understanding.

Frequently that which we do not want to hear is that which we need most to hear. In 2008, four cousins invested a great deal of money in a real estate venture. Their uncle, a man in his 80s with a lifelong record of accomplishment and achievement in business, told them the idea was wrong and the timing was even worse. Their reaction was not positive. They felt that he was being intrusive, offering advice that had not been requested. They also felt that since his outstanding career had been in a different field from real estate, therefore (their words): "What does he know?" Their response to him was none too courteous. They made it clear that if they needed his counsel, they would ask for it. Two years later when the four cousins lost everything, they realized how much they had needed his counsel, how wise it had been, and also how well-intended.

Criticism is not always nor even usually a personal attack. Rather, most of the time it is someone's attempt to guide us in a wise direction. Ego gets in the way. We stiffen and dig our heels in. We defiantly say, "I know what's best!" which is often merely another way of saying, "I know what I have already decided that I want." It never costs us anything to consider an alternative idea about personal plans, nor to listen attentively to constructive critique. At worst, we lose nothing but the time it takes to listen. At best, we stand to gain immeasurably.

There is clearly, however, a dramatic difference between helpful critique and harmful criticism. The latter is an expressed intent to belittle or demean. It doesn't focus on an idea or the performance of a task, but rather on the person who has the idea or performs the task. "You didn't do okay on that" is one thing. "You are not okay" is quite another.

Additionally where critique is concerned, though you should never accept someone's personal denigration, it is usually wise to answer judgment with gracer. The reason is that doing so protects us. We resist taking on and carrying around the weighty burden of resentment. If someone else chooses to be unkind, that is their problem. We do not need to make it our own.

[3] Most of the time, difficult circumstances are temporary. You may be going through a tough time in your life. Focus on the phrase "going through." You're not forever stuck there. You're just going through.

I have no idea what that young mom who danced for her daughter's benefit (far more than for her audience) is doing now. I sincerely suspect she's not dancing in clubs. Her daughter should be in college by this point. Maybe mom is in school, too. Or has secured a degree (or degrees). Or has fallen in love and married? Or has found a different profession or started a business. Of this much, I feel certain, that she almost surely has long since turned her back on the job she hated but endured because of her devotion to her daughter. In retrospect, I suspect she now realizes that her dark night was, in fact, transitory. It was not her forever reality.

Think of your own circumstances. Whatever you are going through as you read this, it is not your forever reality. That's what going "going through" means. You will not stop and reside always in a shadowy place. You can get through this difficult experience, whatever it may be. In fact, you will. It may not feel like it as you trudge along a muddy uphill road of hard times or heartaches. But your current road is not a dead-end. The quality of your future is not determined (and certainly not doomed) by the unfortunate character of your present moment. You've simply got to keep moving so that you can leave where you are and arrive where you need to be. "Yea, though I walk through the valley of the shadow...." (Psalm 23:4)

A rabbi friend in New York told me he often advises people not to think they have to jump over the Red Sea in one giant athletic leap. "Instead," he said, "I counsel people in tough places that they don't have to get past them today. All they have to do right now is to take the next step. And then, the next. And then, the next. In time, all those steps will lead away from the pain and into a new place where they feel alive again."

Were we sitting together in conversation right now you, could probably tell me stories of a dozen people you know (or know about) who seemed stuck in dreary or difficult places. A job, or an endless hunt for the right job. An unhealthy marriage or romantic relationship. Chemical dependency. A challenging illness. Grief. Financial stress. The list is long. You could name those persons and conclude the stories by telling how things ultimately worked out well for many of them. When they were knee-deep in difficulty, they weren't sure that things would ever work out. But, they got through it. They came out on the other side and found the peace, meaning, and joy they had once doubted would ever be their own. We know those people. We know their stories. Thus, we should know that our stories can turn out exactly the same. Tough times are temporary. Better times are yet to come... and, they will.

I hope that life for that dancer-mom has become something so lovely that, in the very best sense of the word, she feels like dancing.

The Honest Woman
In The Wheelchair

"I thank my God with every remembrance of you...."

(Philippians 1:3,

Revised Geneva Translation)

As some people age, for whatever reason, they tend to lose their filters. If a thought enters their heads, it quickly exits their mouths. All of us have been taught by someone when we were growing up that, "Some things ought not be said." Apparently, for numerous folks, in time that lesson is either forgotten or discarded.

An associate and I were walking down a long hallway in a large complex in Greensboro, NC. I had just concluded a speaking engagement there. Well down the hall seated next to the front entrance we spotted a woman who had attended. She was advanced in years, seated in a wheelchair, and apparently waiting for her helper to arrive with transportation. She was beautifully dressed, her hair perfectly coiffed, and sitting high in her seat with an air of self-confidence that defied the purpose of the seat itself. We approached. I greeted her and thanked her for being in the audience that day. In order to make proper eye contact, I bent over from the waist. In so doing, my face was no more than a foot away from hers.

"I've heard you speak several times," she said. "But because of this chair, I always have to sit at the rear of the auditorium. So, we've never met before. Until this moment, I've never actually gotten a good look at you." She studied me silently, then spoke. Her words were clearly unfiltered and, I fear, absolutely accurate. She said, "You know, you look better from a distance." I thought I would need to peel my associate off the floor after he nearly collapsed in a fit of laughter.

I managed to maintain a spirit of cordiality and a smile. We talked for a few minutes more until her ride arrived. If, during that time, she heard my friend trying not to laugh (which only made his laughter worse), she didn't acknowledge it.

"You look better from a distance." Well, what does a person say to that (especially when she was guilty of nothing but telling the truth)?

I simply agreed with her and told her how wise she was on all those previous occasions to just hear me without taking a close look. Thinking back on it, I suspect there may be lessons beyond the obvious humorous one in her remark. Some things do look better from a distance.

Admittedly, the temptation exists to make the past more attractive than it was. "The good old days" also included days when racism, sexism, and exclusivity were accepted as the norms, when certain illnesses that are now easily treatable were considered terminal, when the median income for a year wasn't enough to pay a month's mortgage nowadays, and when life expectancy was less than sixty. Our memory often romanticizes moments in time that were not as grand as we recall them to be. Nonetheless, from a distance, we can see and interpret things more clearly than is sometimes the case up close.

[1] Past events can be interpreted in more helpful and meaningful ways than is possible in the instant when we go through them. What seemed like a disappointment then may later be understood to have been an opportunity for something even better.

I've known numerous people across the years who lost a job only later to discover a career. That would not have occurred, however, had they remained in the previous job. Why? Because they would have had neither the stimulation nor the time required to search for something new. What seemed unsettling in the present moment became a life-transforming positive experience when assessed in retrospect.

A backup quarterback for an NFL team is traded to another team. He didn't see it coming and had neither expressed nor experienced a desire to play elsewhere. But after the trade, he goes from being a backup in one place to a starter (and a star) in the next.

A student cannot handle the strains and pressures of academic life as an eighteen-year-old college freshman. So, he or she drops out and takes a job as a table server in a restaurant. After sufficient time doing that, the former student has matured, has learned by taking on workplace responsibilities, has matured to the point of being able to handle all sorts of responsibilities (including academic), and is, therefore, prepared to attend school with a new sense of determination and enthusiasm. Meanwhile, the former student who had no idea what Major to choose now knows he or she wishes to major in Culinary Arts or Business Administration in order to become a chef or a restaurant owner.

A family moves from a city where they have lived for years. They were familiar with the ebbs and flows of life there. They had established routines that felt safe and secure. They had treasured local friends who enhanced their lives. But for some unexpected reason (a professional assignment, a family issue, etc.), they move to a new and unfamiliar place. Initially, there are feelings of homesickness, anxiety, and loss. But, as time progresses the new place begins to feel less strange. New stores, restaurants, places of worship, schools, and civic and cultural activities become enjoyable and rewarding. The new "house" begins to feel more and more like "home." New friends are discovered who, in time, are as cherished as the ones who were left behind. Later in life, those family members look back, assess, and honestly say, "It was a good move that contributed to a good life. We loved each place, and each made our storehouse of memories rich and rewarding."

As is the case with events, so is it also the case with individuals. From a distance, we sometimes realize that what we originally defined as "the great lost love" (the one who got away) was, in fact, our own very fortunate "great escape." Had that relationship not ended, we would never have met the true love of our lives who has made life for us bright and beautiful beyond measure.

Past events are more accurately interpreted from a distance. In looking back, we often find that the long and winding roads that seemed so difficult to travel at a given moment did at last lead to the destination we had dreamt about.

[2] The impact and influence of people from our yesterdays is enhanced by memory. Think of the parent or grandparent, the teacher or coach, the next-door neighbor or employer who taught you lessons that transformed your very understanding of what it means to be fully alive. Or, think of those persons—even that one single person—who helped you come to know what it means to be fully yourself. When we are in their presence and learning those lessons, we have no way of knowing how valuable the lessons or the teachers are. But when we look back and view it all from a distance, then we know that without them, our lives would have been different and, most likely, diminished.

My mother taught me how to cook, which remains a source of joy and relaxation all these years later. My father, a broadcast journalist and college teacher of Public Speaking, taught me how to use my voice to maximum effectiveness. Mine is not as deep and resonant in the way he was. But, his would say: "There are violins and there are trombones. Each makes music. You learn to play the melody with the instrument you have." Good advice.

Professors like Owen Weatherly, John Carlton, and James M. Efird taught me that there is much to learn, that learning is an adventure, and that it does not conclude with the bestowal of a degree. They each taught me that the better word for cap-and-gown ceremonies is Commencement, not Graduation. A degree is evidence that we have commenced the lifelong adventure of learning, growing, and developing.

Lena Flenniken was my high school English teacher during my senior year. Some thought she was difficult and demanding. Instead, I found her classes to be moments of inspiration. She would stand before us, eyes closed, and quote poetry that obviously transported her to emotional and spiritual places beyond what eyes could not see in that small room. Some of us went on those journeys with her. She inspired within me a love of poetry which even still can take me to faraway places of mystery and magic.

Someone said to each of us, "I believe in you." Someone said, "You can do this," or "You can do more." Someone indicated through word or deed that we do not face life alone, that purpose and meaning can be found, that "settling for" is never as noble as "dreaming of," that we can be agents for good (i.e., parts of the solution rather than parts of the problem), and that around each corner may await the potential for happiness that can be ours if we refuse to give up but instead keep believing and moving forward. We couldn't fully appreciate those people in the moment. But looking back from a distance, we see clearly what they were to us then... as well as how their memories and lessons remain with us now.

[3] Moments that once brought tears later on can bring smiles. Especially in seasons of grief when the wound of loss is fresh and deep, smiles are difficult to come by. Most memories initially cause us to lament what was and what we feel can be no more, reminding us of one who is "gone." But given enough time, those very same memories remind us that he is not gone or that she is still near.

A friend whose husband died in a tragic fashion and at a premature age put away her photos of him. Especially difficult, she said, were the family photos. There he was, smiling while holding their children in his arms or while holding her. "I couldn't look at the pictures without feeling the searing pain of loss," she told me. "He should be here with those arms still wrapped around those of us he loved," she thought with each glance at a framed memory. "But, he is not. Nor will he be again. The photos were painful reminders of what was lost." Two years have passed. Little by little she has learned to look at the photos again and has even placed some of them here and there around her house. She says now they are more sources of comfort than pain. "They no longer remind me so much of what was lost," she said, "but rather of what was. And what was, was good. I wouldn't have missed it for the world. It didn't last as long as I had hoped, but it was real and it brought joy while it did last. Now, those memories are beginning to bring joy again."

Looking back from a distance changes our perspective. Whether the topic is people who were in our lives for a season until we both moved in different directions, people who loved us (and we them) but love did not last, or people whose lives ended, the initial sense of loss in time becomes a new sense of awareness. We become aware that for whatever time we intersected, they were sources of something good to us, and we are better for that experience. We become aware that painful endings do not negate the beauties that preceded them. And we often learn that the impact and influence of their lives live on with us and in us, even if the people do not. Moments that once brought tears later on can bring smiles.

[4] Having survived tough times gives us the courage to face new challenges. Often we hear someone say, "I didn't think I could get through it, but I did." Whatever the crisis or challenge happens to be, we humans are endowed with a remarkable capacity for survival. That does not mean that tough times become easy. It simply means that we are stronger than they are. We can withstand, process, and move forward. To be sure, we often move forward with scars and sadness. But still, we move forward. One day at a time, one step at a time, we survive and proceed.

Looking back from a distance at those times encourages when other difficult moments occur. "I didn't think I could make it through that," we say. "But I did. Therefore, I know I can make it through this, too!" And we do.

The illustrations are timeworn and clichéd, perhaps, but still true. Edison did fail a thousand times before he finally succeeded in making an electric bulb light. Colonel Sanders was rejected dozens of times before finding someone who would take a risk on his recipe for fried chicken. Kathryn Stockett was rejected by over sixty literary agents before one decided to try to get her book called The Help published. That book went on to sell over ten million copies and was produced as an award-winning movie. Elvis Presley was fired after his first live performance and was told, "You need to go back to driving a truck." Each of those persons (and thousands of other successful folks like them) discovered the courage to move forward, courage that is born from surviving disappointments in the past. "If I could make it through that" are seven words that arm us for surviving and often even triumphing.

Additionally, memories of making it through tough times remind us of the importance of loving shoulders to lean on. In almost every shadowy circumstance through which we pass, there is someone who steps forward to help us face what we did not desire to face. There is some person who hangs in there with us, loves us, listens to us, holds us up when otherwise we might fall, and faithfully points out glimmers of light that remind us all is not darkness. In remembering those individuals who were there with us, beside us, and for us, our confidence in human nature is strengthened. Whatever bad things we may read in the news about humanity, we know from experience that there are good things and good people, as well. All hope is not lost as long as those individuals exist. We maintain hope in the face of any trials because we know they need not be faced alone. Looking back from a distance, we discover courage via past challenges and memories of people who helped us face them.

[5] Life is good. It really does look better from a distance when we can view what has happened thus far in its totality. The urgency of that which is immediate sometimes obscures that.

The labors of college and grad school are intense. None who take education seriously can deny that. Those who desire to learn and achieve recognize that becoming educated requires work. It doesn't come easily, nor should it. I often remind students in my university classes that AI can write their papers but cannot help them learn, nor can it prepare them to succeed on a final exam when ChatGPT can't help you figure out which of the multiple-choice answers is the correct one. You can swim the Lazy River and manage somehow to receive a degree. But to receive an education, you have to fight your way through the rapids. The final result, however, is that however difficult med school was, the surgeon who succeeded now practices medicine and saves lives. However demanding receiving a Bachelor's or Master's in Education may have been, the teacher who did the work required now educates young people and provides them the opportunity for full and rewarding lives. Law schools, theological schools, business schools, etc., are rarely easy rides. But they lead to desired and meaningful destinations. In looking back, we realize that what seemed difficult in a long-ago moment resulted in joy and purpose later on. Furthermore, most of us look back and can see the full picture, which included not only the long hours in libraries and labs and the stressful exams and term papers but also friends and parties and romances and warm Saturday afternoons at the football stadium with our classmates. When we assess things from a distance, it's hard not to see beauty in addition to difficulties. It's hard not to come to the conclusion that in spite of the tough times, life is good.

My first job after graduation was in a small North Carolina mill town. I lived in (but did not own) a nice little brick house. My roommate was a Saint Bernard. My salary was $7700 a year, probably 20% of which was annually required to keep my 1971 Pinto road-worthy. Few people knew my name. I had written no books and had appeared on no network specials. But in the four years I lived there, I was introduced to the most loving and nurturing people imaginable. My next-door-neighbors looked after me as if I were one of their own children, at least two or three nights a week inviting me over for home-cooked meals. A couple not far from where I lived had a large garden behind their house. In warm weather, they harvested every imaginable vegetable, many of which they canned for winter. Every Wednesday they would place on my doorstep four or five meals in Styrofoam containers. They were the leftovers from their meals the night before. I made lifelong friends in that community. I learned lessons about hope amid hard times from those who worked long hours in the mill but found meaning and joy in family, community, faith, and the arts. Being there set in motion the journey that ultimately led me to New York City and all the doors that opened in there. Without the former, I doubt I would have experienced the latter. Much of what my life is now was born in that small community off the beaten path with warm and loving people who taught me about life and how it is good (especially when we are good in our treatment of others).

Not merely in looking back, of course, but also in looking around we are able to see blessings and beauties. They are there every day if we simply pay attention. However, it is often the looking back from a distance that clarifies how blessed and beautiful (or simply, how important) things really were. As we remember and assess, we realize the inherent goodness of life. In so doing, we likewise come to understand that if life has been good in the past, there is undeniable potential that it can be likewise in the present and the future.

"You look better from a distance," said the honest woman in the wheelchair. I'm sure that is true where my appearance is concerned. I'm also sure it is true about the greater topic of life itself.

Hotel Rooms And Side Streets

"Consider well the lilies of the field... Not even Solomon in all his glory was arrayed as one of these."

(Matthew 6:28-29,
Young's Literal Translation)

On my third day at a convention in St. Louis, I found myself with most of the morning free. So, rather than eating the continental fare in the hotel dining area, I opted to go next door to a Bob Evans Restaurant where I could indulge myself in ravenous gluttony over a stack of cherry pancakes. My rationale was that (a) I would eat a light lunch and (b) I would go to the fitness center later that day. Deep down I knew that Point A was unlikely and Point B simply was not going to happen. I was, however, undeterred by that as I sat down to devour a stack of sugar and carbs baptized with a thorough drenching of cherries and maple syrup.

My table server was a native of the city and proud of it. A couple minutes after taking my order, she reappeared with a coffee refill. "What are you doing in St. Louis?" she asked. I replied that I was part of a convention being held at the hotel next door. Polite conversation ensued, mostly consisting of my explaining what the convention was about and why I was in attendance.

After courteously enduring my monologue, she posed another question: "How much touring around have you done in your free time?" I replied that there really hadn't been much free time and, thus, I had done no touring at all.

"This is a great city," she countered.

"I'm sure it is," I answered. "My mom's brother and her first cousin played baseball here. They were both catchers. They loved St. Louis."

"You'd love it, too," she said, "if you would take a look at it. But, you can't see St. Louis from a hotel room."

The table server was spot on with that advice. It reminded me of an experience I had in Paris. My wife has traveled there on numerous occasions and adores it. Many of my friends go regularly and enthusiastically extol its beauties and virtues. For whatever reason, of all the places I have traveled, I have been to Paris only once, and that was just for an hour. The hour was spent in the Charles de Gaulle Airport during a layover on a flight to Istanbul.

Have I been to Paris? Yes. Have I seen it? No. Because you can't see Paris from an airport. Nor can you see St. Louis from a hotel room. Nor can you see the best, brightest, and most beautiful parts of life by standing still. So, let me share this traveler's takeaway: **To find the best in life, we have to go looking for it**. Things worth finding rarely come to us. Almost always, we have to seek them out.

One of the best ways to find life's treasures is to look where not everyone else is looking. A few summers ago, I was honored to keynote and make a couple of additional presentations at a national administrators' conference, which met at the Convention Center in New Orleans. My wife accompanied me on that trip so that in addition to the work I was doing, we could also take advantage of the playground called "the Big Easy."

One evening, we wandered through the French Quarter in search of a place to have dinner. Lines stretched outside some of the more famous and touristy spots. Because of that, we kept wandering until we turned onto a street off the main thoroughfare and then took yet another small street off of it. There we found private residences, boutiques, a couple of art galleries, and an absence of the high traffic and noise we had experienced only a few blocks away. Walking past what appeared to be a lovely old two-story home (French architecture, white paint, and a beautiful narrow iron fence around the lot), our eyes were drawn to a lighted room at the front of the house. There we spotted several people seated at dining tables.

"My goodness," my wife spoke up, "that's not a home. It's a restaurant tucked away on this little street. Maybe we ought to check it out." So we did, and in so doing, discovered one of the finest meals we have ever eaten in one of the most delightful settings we have ever visited. The service was extraordinary. The food was delicious. The presentation would easily qualify as fine art. The chef, as it turned out, was the author of numerous books on French-American cuisine. It was a totally enjoyable evening.

A friendly couple seated at the table next to ours asked if we enjoyed our meal. We quickly replied with enthusiasm about the quality of everything we had experienced there from the very moment we walked through the door. Our neighbors seemed pleased and told us that they were locals who had been dining at that restaurant for years. They gave us a brief bio about the chef/owner who had carved out her own place of high respect in the culinary world of New Orleans. At one point, describing the restaurant's delicious fare and faithful clientele, one of them said, "This place may be off the beaten path in this city. But, on the side streets, you'll find the real treasures."

"On the side streets, you'll find the real treasures." Life says a bold "Amen" to that. Sometimes it is where we least expect a blessing that the greatest blessings show up. A simple friendship that turns into something more, and romantic love unexpectedly blooms... a temporary job that excites us in ways we had not imagined and becomes a long-term career... a class we took in undergraduate school just to gain three more hours' credit but stirred our imagination in such fashion that it became a lifelong passion... a small investment we made in a startup which did not seem promising but years later provided incredible returns... a pet we relented to accept only because our spouse or children wanted it, but in time it became one of the greatest and most loyal companions we ever knew... a movie we watched out of boredom that stimulated thoughts and visions which helped shape who we later became... a choice we made to listen to someone who was lonely even though we were in a hurry, and the incomparable life lesson we learned by hearing what they had to say. All those things and countless others like them are side streets. They are actions we took without having great expectations, but in the final tally they surprised us with things of lasting value. "On the side streets, you'll find the real treasures." To find the best in life, we have to go looking for it. And, one of the places to look that is filled with unanticipated potential is frequently on life's side streets.

You can't see St. Louis from a hotel room. You can't see Paris from an airport. You can't see New Orleans if you only walk down Bourbon Street. And you can't find life by sitting still or remaining in your closed or comfortable confines.

The truth is that beauty, joy, meaningful relationships, and genuine love do not respect any confines. They may exist there. But they do not exist only there.

A man I know who has evolved in an impressive way readily admits that he grew up as a racist. He was not hostile toward those of other races. But he was exclusive of them. He had been reared in a home where prejudice, as is usually the case, was born of fear that was the result of ignorance. When we know nothing about others, we tend to be intimidated by them. When we grow intimidated by (afraid of) others, prejudice is almost inevitably the result. So it had been in his home as a youth, and he had adopted (more or less by osmosis) the bigotry of his parents.

While serving in the military, the man had been stationed in California (almost three thousand miles from his home). Christmas holidays came around, and he was not able to fly back to be with family. So, it appeared he was doomed to remain on a nearly empty base enduring the holiday with a handful of other soldiers who were little more than strangers to him. However, a young man whose bunk was near his own and whom he only knew casually, extended an invitation: "Why don't you spend Christmas Day with my family? We live six miles from here. There will be lots of people, lots of food, laughter, and music. It will be better than staying in this barracks alone."

The man extending the invitation was African American. The man I know had been reared in a home that intentionally chose not to interact with people of color. This would be a totally new experience for him. Whatever his reason—loneliness, a holiday-induced crack in his emotional armor, a previously unacknowledged suspicion that his prejudice was ill-founded, etc.—he accepted the invitation.

Christmas Day that year was a transformative experience for the young soldier. He was welcomed with graciousness and unfeigned hospitality by people whom he had been taught to reject. He was treated to a festival of faith and kindness. Someone who had never met him had even gone out and bought gifts for him so that when family members unwrapped their presents, he would not be left out. Later he would say, "Of all the Christmases I have spent across the years, that was the best of all."

How did his story turn out? Hollywood couldn't have created a better script. He and the soldier who had invited him to a holiday visit in his home became like family to one another. They remain lifelong friends who still refer to one another as "brothers." The young man's epiphany, which began that Christmas Day in the presence of kind and caring strangers, gave birth to a spirit of inclusivity and a passion to break down walls of racial prejudice. He has made that his life's avocation. On his mantle is a photo of him with his old friend, all smiles at a wedding where one of their grandsons married one of their granddaughters.

Let me reiterate: Beauty, joy, meaningful relationships, and genuine love do not respect our confines. We often find the best life has to offer in places we had not planned to look... and in people we had been hesitant to embrace. The point is that life at its best is bigger than whatever our personal parameters are. To find and experience life that is that full and enriching requires that we stretch our boundaries... that we move in the direction of what we hope to discover because it rarely just comes to us... and that we travel side streets and remain open to the great serendipities of living.

A friend of mine says he begins each morning with the same questions, which he poses to himself in the mirror as he shaves: "What do you want? What steps will you take today to find it?" You can't see St. Louis from a hotel room. So said a wise table server at breakfast in Bob Evans. Whatever you want most in life, you have to go out in search of it. Be strategic. Be diligent. And while on your search, don't rush past the side streets.

The Walker in the Mall

"Therefore encourage one another and build one another up."

(I Thessalonians 5:11,

Revised Standard Version)

I enjoy working out at the Y. That could be better (and more accurately) expressed. I "endure" working out at the Y so that I can "enjoy" the benefit... which is to increase my daily caloric intake. I "endure" so that I can "indulge" which means the end result is that I "enjoy." There. That is properly stated.

Not everyone goes to the Y. I like the variety of machines they provide. My wife prefers just doing Pilates on a reformer for a couple of hours. Some folks simply walk in the mall. I get that. Often I choose the mall instead of the Y.

I was in the mall recently looking for a wall calendar. As I walked toward the Hallmark Store, I happened to fall in stride beside a man who was there simply for the exercise. "Getting your 10,000 steps," he asked. Feeling no need to explain my Y routine or desire for a calendar, I simply answered, "Yes."

He continued. "I come here every day. I get up early each morning and have my Special K and a banana. Then I come to the mall and try to do a minimum of 12,000-15,000 steps. I'm eating better. I'm exercising like I never did when I worked full-time. I've lost over 30 pounds." I congratulated him.

"You know," he said, "back when I began this routine, I would tire out after 1,000 steps. Seriously. 1,000 steps. That's not quite half a mile. Now on a good day I can 20,000 or more and not even get winded." More kudos from me... along with an escape plan to make my way to Hallmark. I didn't know him. I am by nature a bit of an introvert. I had been thrust into a conversation with a stranger about a topic that seemed pretty quickly exhausted. Where's Hallmark?

"Yes sir," he went on, "I am healthier than I've been in years. I'm living better and will probably live longer... and I have no idea why."

That last statement threw me, and apparently it showed. He smiled, but it wasn't a happy smile. Just a knowing one. "You tell me," he said. "Why am I taking steps to live such a long and healthy life? My wife died five years ago. My children are grown and have moved away. One of them I never hear from. I'm retired, so I have no real sense of purpose anymore. Every day I just get up, eat my cereal, come to the mall and walk by myself, then go home to an empty apartment to wait until tomorrow morning when I will do it all over again. My life has been reduced to that."

We stepped on for a moment, enveloped in silence. I felt the need to respond, though I wasn't quite sure how. It wasn't like he was tuning in to watch me on PBS or something, hoping for motivation and inspiration. I was just a stranger in the local mall who happened to be walking beside him. What was I supposed to say?

"Well," I began, "since you did say 'You tell me,' let me take a stab at it. Maybe you're living healthier and will live longer because there are people who love and need you. Just because your children are grown and living in distant places doesn't mean they don't want contact with their dad. And, who knows when or how you and your silent child will reconnect? Onc thing is for sure—If you were not around, then reconnecting would be impossible. You're retired? Okay. But why should that translate into a lack of purpose? There must be a hundred different volunteer opportunities here in our community. You are a person with a professional track record and a lifetime of experience. I'm betting there are countless ways you could use that to help people. And, you have no way of knowing what the future holds for you right around the next corner, or the one after that or after that. Who knows the new friendships and relationships, the new adventures that await you?"

Again we walked without talking. By now I had passed the Hallmark store, but it didn't matter. I could use the extra steps required to circle back to it. Anyway, it felt more important for me to continue being present for a stranger as he pondered the meaning of his life than it was to find the right wall calendar for my office.

At last he spoke. "You believe all that?"

"Yes sir, I do," I answered.

"What if you're wrong, and there's nothing out there for me?"

"What if I'm right and there is, but you check out before you find it?"

"I guess something down deep in me believes it, too," he replied with a muted chuckle, "or else I wouldn't bother coming here and counting my steps. You know, I've thought about coming a half hour earlier and joining the group of walkers. But I don't know any of them."

"If you walk with them, you'll get to know them in a hurry," I told him. "And walking with friends is probably a lot more enjoyable than walking alone."

My takeaway is that **the future is worth striving for, and often the benefits we find along the way in the journey are the greatest blessings of all.**

We fell silent again. I couldn't think of anything more to say. So I excused myself at that point, turning back toward Hallmark. As I walked away, he called out, "You're right. Walking with a friend is a lot more enjoyable than walking alone. At least, it has been this morning." With that, I walked a little taller.

Don't You Just Love The Rain?

"He has shown kindness by giving you rain...."

(Acts 14:17,

New International Version)

Recently I ran across an essay I composed quite a few years ago. I'm not sure why I wrote it originally. Maybe it had to do with nothing more than the fact that I was apparently enjoying a day off in the city where I then lived and which I deeply loved. Maybe there was some other purpose. Was it intended to become a blog or part of a book I was writing? In truth, I'm not really sure. Nor does it matter much, I suppose. The point is that I wrote it, filed it away where I would not lose it, and promptly forgot it was there. Today I found it, several years after it was written. In re-reading it, I realize how glad I am it was not used for whatever its original purpose may have been.

That's because it needs to be here, in this book on this topic. This rediscovered essay was based on a momentary encounter I had with a woman walking her dog in the rain. Reading what I wrote then, I experienced an unexpected encounter with myself—at least, with the self I was at that point in time. Here's what I wrote.

This is my New York. Every citizen here has his or her own version. This is mine. It has not always been as soothing as it is now. Initially there were inevitable adjustments moving from a mid-sized town in the south to bigger-than-life Manhattan. It seemed strange once upon a time. But given time, it began to feel like home.

Through no real desire of her own, for almost a decade my wife has had to live in two worlds. One is here with me for about eight months a year. The other is five hundred miles away, where we have children who need a parent and she has an aging parent who needs her daughter. It hasn't been easy on my wife. She is back and forth constantly—two weeks there, three weeks here. She's done the best she knows how to do, trying to keep everyone happy. In the process, for almost ten years she has never quite known which place to call "home."

Do I miss her? Of course. But I will see her again soon. Do I miss my children so far away?

I do. But I will also see them again soon. And in truth, they are grown now. I have come to understand that I probably miss them more than they do me. They have their lives, their primary relationships, their homes and jobs (as they should). No longer do they need Daddy in the same way they once did.

The absences are not always easy, nor would I desire them for long periods of time. And yet, a fair amount of the time this is what my life is like. You find your rhythm. You learn to deal with whatever your reality happens to be. Eventually, it begins to feel comfortable. At least, it feels less and less uncomfortable. Later still, it begins to feel natural. Today I am alone, and it's okay. This is my New York.

Today is Friday, the day I take off from work. No tie. No jacket. No meetings. No phone calls. On days like these when she is away tending to the other half of her life, by choice I am around virtually no other people at all. I used to feel guilty about that. After all, this is New York City... the Big Apple... the city that never sleeps... the place with a million things to do, whichever directions your tastes may run. So, for a while I felt almost compelled not to miss what the city has to offer, to be out and about and doing, whether or not that was what I desired. Now I no longer feel so compelled.

This is my New York, this quiet Friday world where I can bathe myself in solitude. Were I to walk only two blocks west, I would be surrounded by the traffic, noise, and the rapid pace that is the New York of so many others. But this lovely apartment tucked away on a cul-de-sac is my oasis from all that. There are flowers on the terrace and birds that come and go. I like to think this is their oasis, too. When weather permits, I can sit with my early-morning coffee on that terrace and watch the boats go by on the East River, wondering where they came from and where they are bound. My imagination about all that is enough for me. I don't really need answers. It calms me just to sit and sip, to watch and wonder.

Today it's raining. I've come to enjoy rain on Fridays. It helps me justify my tendency to withdraw from the busy world two blocks away. "I would be out today," I tell myself, "visiting museums or getting lunch or listening to music in a jazz club or just walking through the Village. But of course, I can't be out because it's raining." A perfect excuse to justify my desire for quiet. Today I ventured out only far enough to purchase tomatoes and Banza (a wonderful thing for those of us who do not want to give up pasta but have decided to restrict carbs). Making my way back to our apartment building, I encountered a woman walking her dogs. She had no umbrella. Her hair and clothing were wet from the weather. And yet, she appeared to be in no hurry at all. As I was about to go down the steps toward our front door, she smiled at me and said, "Don't you just love the rain?" She was guessing, I suppose. She guessed correctly. The rain has given me a guilt-free chance to remain here in this relaxing place all day, this still and safe place where I can just be.

And so I have settled into my lovely Friday world, watching the rain bounce off the terrace to the courtyard below where it becomes one with so many other raindrops that have formed a tiny, shimmering pond. Across the FDR freeway I see other raindrops falling and becoming one with the East River. I treated myself to a movie-on-demand. This Beautiful Fantastic is one of those wonderfully acted and filmed British pieces that is in no hurry to tell its story. There are no guns, no car chases, no nudity, and no international intrigue. But there are people who you get to know as the film progresses, little by little, one layer of the onion at a time, until the end comes and you have made four new friends you didn't know when the movie began. There is also a book on the table that I began reading only yesterday. Today the rain gives me permission to stay inside and spend time reading more. In the background, my Pandora plays spa music. Campy? Absolutely. But to me, it is also comforting. This quiet, thoughtful, unhurried oasis is my New York.

I will be busy again soon. Tomorrow morning at 9:00, I have a speaking engagement at the Yale Club. The next morning at 11:00, I will preach at Marble Collegiate Church on a busy and bustling corner where 5th Avenue connects with W. 29th Street. Monday is another speaking engagement. Tuesday I film. There are four meetings this week that I would pay good money to avoid, but I am required to attend (though I sincerely doubt the outcome of those meetings would in any way be altered if I failed to show). There is business to attend to. Appointments to keep. Phone calls to make, and emails to answer. I will be on buses and subways. I will tread the crowded sidewalks shoulder-to-shoulder with thousands of strangers in a hurry to arrive somewhere. That is the New York where I work and seek to make a difference in the lives of others.

But today, there will be no speaking engagements or meetings or buses or sidewalks or emails to answer. Today is Friday. I am alone, and it is raining. That gives me the welcome (in fact, beautiful) opportunity to remain inside with the boats and the birds and my thoughts and my music in my New York.

We're not all wired the same. A friend whom I admire and respect borders on being frenetic. He simply cannot remain still. He knows he is that way and that he is unlikely ever to be any other way. When I tease him about it, he simply laughs and replies, "Man, I just don't want to miss anything!" I respect that. As for me, though, there are times like today when what I don't want to miss is silence, stillness, and solitude that become treasures to savor on stress-free days like this.

It's Friday. I am allowed to remain in my apartment with no guilt at all because of the weather outside. "Don't you just love the rain?"

That's where the essay concluded. As I re-read it now, I discover some brief takeaways. [1] **One is that we do not always choose (or even prefer) our circumstances, but we can learn to make the best of them**. My wife and I did not prefer being apart as much as we were. But, we learned to make it work. In fact, perhaps the previous sentence should have ended four words earlier than it did. "We learned."

We learned at a new and deeper level that everyone   has   multiple   interpersonal commitments. And they are not in competition. You cannot (and should not) invest all your time or love in one single other person, however central that person may be to your life. Instead, you and I create ways of honoring the lives of all who look to us and lean on us. The multiple commitments, while sometimes logistically exhausting, are also essentially life-enhancing. We love spouses and friends, parents and children, and in loving all we learn to love each one in a more authentic and particular way.

We learned that a new experience, if consistently repeated, will become a pattern that is your norm. Whether or not that norm was desired, as previously noted, we humans have a remarkable capacity for creating new rhythms. While in North Carolina, my wife had time to sharpen her skills as a gardener. She also had a large fenced-in backyard space that was not size-limited to a small terrace in the inner city. Thus, she has been able to create a relatively expansive visual masterpiece with flowers and shrubs of all descriptions, fountains, brick walkways through the greenery, a haven for birds and butterflies, squirrels and chipmunks. The hobby brings her joy, and the ambiance brings equal joy to all who see it. Meanwhile, I discovered forms of theater that she and I did not attend together.

With one another, we went to Broadway plays, especially musicals. It was something we loved doing as a couple. When she was away, however, I discovered how much I personally enjoyed attending Off-Broadway shows, and Off-Off Broadway, as well. Every August, I was a devotee of Fringe Theater, that wonderful NYC experience where young playwrights and actors test their wares in front of small audiences in black box playhouses. On some Fridays or Saturdays, I would attend three plays in a single day, losing myself in the joy of imagination and the peace of watching someone else work.

We learned that time apart provides space to reflect on relationships—on what areas are hitting on all cylinders and what others need to be tended like those flowers in her backyard garden. Reunions are sweet when people have been apart for an extended period. Time together is not so likely taken for granted.

Fill in your own blank. A friendship moves in a direction you had not planned. A job that you had hoped would be a career turns, instead, into a challenge. Your best friends who lived next door for forty years move away, and strangers move in. The composition of your family unit (either immediate or extended) is altered in some unexpected fashion. The list goes on and on. Everyone can name some experiences that were unplanned (often undesired) and yet are real. When those occasions come, we have two options: either we sulk or we grow. We can curse the thorns or smell the roses. Life happens. It's what we do with what happens that makes life terrible or livable.

[2] Another takeaway is that what we so often interpret as misfortune may, in fact, pave the way for good fortune. A friend I know has a friend who was a Wall Street financier. During the recession of 2009, he fell victim to downsizing. He went from making a head-spinning salary to making none at all, with a family to support, a mortgage to pay, and a child in college with tuition bills that arrived irrespective of his income or lack thereof. The man fell into a very real (and very understandable) depression. One afternoon his teenage daughter walked into the den where her father sat silent and gloomy.

"Dad," she said, "have you looked at the bright side of this."

Not so much with irritation as with resignation bordering on despair, he answered, "There is no bright side."

"I think there is," she continued, "if you're willing to see it."

Then she reminded him of how all her life he had complained of the stresses of his job, the long hours and high expectations. She also reminded him that his lifelong dream was not to invest other people's money but to be a baker. That conversation ignited a series of conversations including the man, his wife, that daughter, and their son in college.

What followed were two years of a journey that was admittedly difficult. But, the end result was that the man and his family rented space and opened a small bakery in Brooklyn. It became a family business. Mom and Dad worked together every day. The kids joined in on most weekends. The business developed a loyal clientele, eventually resulting in the opening of additional satellite outlets. The man told my friend that he had lost a good living but had found a good life.

Things are not always as we would have designed them. When that is the case, what new design can we create that will bring joy and meaning we had never dreamt about?

[3] The third takeaway is that as hard and as fast as we are often forced to push ahead in life, occasionally it is medicinal and

restorative to pull back. Religious communities refer to this principle as Shabbat (Sabbath). It simply means that without rest, we will eventually wear out.

If I were to do a cross-country drive from my home in North Carolina to visit friends in Oregon or California, no matter what long hours I spent on the interstates daily nor how fast I drove, times would come when I would have to stop and refuel. Cars cannot drive when the tank is empty. Neither can people. If we do not sit still from time to time, we will not remain able to properly move forward. We will run out of gas. My rainy day Fridays were occasions for refueling. My life is busy, and I love that. But, there come moments when the busyness demands that I step away from it in order to "restore my soul" (Psalm 23:3) for stepping back into it.

So, my advice to everyone (i.e., to you) is to find what you love to do, that which brings you happiness and peacefulness, and do more of it. It may be biking or hiking, golfing or gardening, going to plays or playing with your grandkids. It may simply be creating a quiet place for a day of rest, reading, and watching the world go by. It may be one of a hundred different things. Whatever it is, make room for it. If we don't take care of ourselves, the time will come when there won't be enough self left to take proper care of anyone or anything else.

As I write this, outside my window I see a soft pouring of water from the skies, washing away the dust and grime that accumulates. It is making the world clean again. And it is causing me to say, "Don't you just love the rain?"

One More Takeaway

"Pay attention to what you are taught, and you will be successful."

(Proverbs 16:20,

Good News Translation)

This has happened to me so many times that I could never begin to accurately estimate the number. I conclude a sermon or speech and as I am greeting members of the audience afterward, someone takes my hand, is kind and complimentary, and asks, "How do you manage to meet so many interesting people? Where on earth do you find all those stories?" My answer is always the same. "I just pay attention."

That's it. No magic. No mystery. No monkish mastery of life's hidden wisdom. I just pay attention to the people around me. I watch them. I listen to them. Inevitably by doing just that much, almost every day people teach me life lessons of unimaginable importance.

I did not orchestrate any of the encounters reported in this book. I just happened to be in the right place at the right time and observed life.

Probably the modern-day Willy Loman on a subway landing would have spoken his exhausted word to whomever looked him in the eye. I just happened to be the one to whom he did so. When he spoke, I listened.

Had I not stepped onto the elevator at exactly the moment I did, in all likelihood the anxious young woman would have found the right floor and our paths would not have crossed. But I happened to share her space at that precise moment. When she reacted to me in what seemed an odd way, I observed and imagined what might have been behind her reaction.

The blind man who saw a deeper meaning in Christmas decorations than I could see with 20/20 vision would doubtless have shared his special insights with others in front of the Lord and Taylor windows had I walked on by. But instead, I paused at a precise moment to view the holiday wonder. Thus, I became the one to whom that man revealed a beauty deeper than

I had been able to perceive. We met by happenstance, but when it occurred, I listened.

The table servers in St. Louis and New Orleans... the child with a bubble maker on a busy city street corner... the aged dancer with a collection of photos... the disillusioned student reading a newspaper... the women walking their dogs... the kind young man on a street corner in Harlem... and all the others I mentioned in this book brought light and understanding to my life that had not previously been there. Those people basically just happened to me. A normal day was in process. It was nothing special or out of the ordinary at all. But then, around a corner, someone appeared. A statement was made. A deed was observed. A gesture of kindness was extended. And a window in my mind opened that would never shut again. Life changed for me because of those unexpected encounters.

Here's the takeaway: **As many people appear around the corners in your life as do in mine. So, pay attention.** I regularly tell my students that the secret to making a good grade is to "Pay attention and take notes." Some take me seriously. When grades are posted, it's always clear that some others did not. What I say to them, I write to you. Pay attention. Watch. Listen. Remember. And, take notes.

Here's a suggestion: Keep a People Journal. In a teenager's diary, most entries are about people. Sure, on occasion the young person will write something down about a pet or a movie recently seen. But the vast majority of that which is written has to do with the individuals who populate the young person's world. They write about encounters. Relationships (or the dream for relationships). Someone hurt her. Someone scorned him. Someone complimented him. Someone flirted with her. Someone is struggling. Someone else is funny. Every entry is about something critical to the young person's life. And most are reflections about other people. We busy adults can learn a lot from the wisdom of youth.

When you have an encounter that brings insight or inspiration, write it down. Include as many details as possible. Then, at the end of each month, read your entries from the past thirty days. After a year or so of doing that, what you have seen, heard, remembered, and reflected on from others will have made you a different person than you were before.

My dad was a great storyteller. As a journalist, he met and interviewed a large number of singularly interesting people in the course of his long career. When he was well into his 80s, I asked him if he would write down the stories he sometimes told.

He replied, "Who would be interested in reading what I write?"

I answered, "I would be. Your grandchildren would be. It's part of your legacy, and something we cherish and want to keep."

Eventually he relented, leaving us a volume of fascinating stories he recalled in print—all of them encounters with people from famous athletes to entertainers, from politicians to Sitting Bull's grandson remembering walking Little Big Horn with his grandfather the day after the battle. The written stories are more valuable than diamonds and pearls to those of us who loved him. But, here's something interesting. After Dad completed writing the stories, he said, "Every one of these reminded me of something timeless."

Life is a series of stories. The truly timeless ones come in the form of encounters. We unexpectedly bump into someone, often a stranger. They say or do something that has an immediate impact. However, the impact can be misplaced or forgotten if not recorded. Life with all its demands and responsibilities lays its claims at our doorsteps. And they often arrive with senses of immediacy and urgency. We do not (and sometimes cannot) take time to merely reflect on things. So, a "pearl of great price" (Matthew 13:46) is forgotten. That's the beauty of a People Journal. We record impactful moments. Even if we don't have time just then to ponder them carefully, turning them in our hands like a priceless stone, seriously considering every facet, when we do have time, we can open the pages and read. And remember. And relive experiences. And learn life lessons that otherwise would be forgotten.

Every day is a classroom, and what we witness therein is our textbook. From the beauty parlor to the grocery store to the golf course to the playground to the city park to the community garden, from the church to the synagogue to the mosque to the meditation center, from the bookstore to the coffee shop to the civic club to the fitness center, wherever we find others, we find lessons about life. Valuable lessons. Indispensable lessons. Lasting lessons that come through chance encounters.

So, don't miss the magic. Don't become so overwhelmed by the busyness of life that you fail to experience the beauty of living. We get one chance at this. If we pay attention, take notes, and learn what is there to be learned, then we won't squander the chance we were given.

Instead we will discover something rich with adventure, meaning, and joy. It's called Living. It's really far too good to be missed.

About the Author

Michael Brown is an author (his numerous books include *The Love Principle* and *A Long Ago Birth in a Right Now World*), has been on the faculties of High Point, Duke, and Wake Forest Universities and New Brunswick Theological School, is a motivational speaker, and for ten years was Senior Minister at Marble Collegiate Church on 5th Avenue in New York City. He has been featured in national television specials on ABC, NBC, and PBS. His is a message of hope, positivity, and transformational faith, calling us to determine our own pathways to meaningful lives.